INTRODUCTION
to the
PENTATEUCH

INTRODUCTION
to the
PENTATEUCH

R. N. Whybray

WILLIAM B. EERDMANS PUBLISHING COMPANY
GRAND RAPIDS, MICHIGAN

ISBN 0-8028-0837-9

Scripture quotations are from the *New Revised Standard Version of the Bible* ©
1989 by the Division of Christian Education, National Council of the Churches
of Christ in the United States of America, used by permission.

Note: Biblical references are given as in modern English Bibles rather than as in
Hebrew Bibles, where the verse numbers sometimes differ slightly.

Contents

Abbreviations

AB	Anchor Bible
ANET	*Ancient Near Eastern Texts Relating to the Old Testament,* ed. J. B. Pritchard (Princeton: Princeton University Press, 1950, ³1969)
BA	*Biblical Archaeologist*
BZAW	Beihefte zur *Zeitschrift für die Alttestamentliche Wissenschaft*
CBQ	*Catholic Biblical Quarterly*
CBSC	Cambridge Bible for Schools and Colleges
ICC	International Critical Commentary
JBL	*Journal of Biblical Literature*
JSOT	*Journal for the Study of the Old Testament*
NCBC	New Century Bible Commentary
NRSV	New Revised Standard Version
OTG	Old Testament Guides
OTL	Old Testament Library
RB	*Revue Biblique*
REB	Revised English Bible
SBT	Studies in Biblical Theology
SNTS	Studiorum Novi Testamenti Societas
VT	*Vetus Testamentum*
VTS	Supplements to *Vetus Testamentum*
WBC	Word Biblical Commentary

Preface

I<small>N THIS TEXTBOOK</small>, distinguished biblical scholar R. Norman Whybray provides a straightforward and insightful introduction to the background, content, and themes of one of the major portions of the biblical corpus. This entry-level resource for colleges and seminaries strives to make sense of major critical issues in a field where new and conflicting theories abound, by not only surveying recent studies but also introducing students to the major contributions of earlier scholars that have brought biblical studies to this point. Boldy delineating and analyzing the cutting edge of current literary, historical, and sociological approaches to biblical criticism, the author stresses the intention and meaning of the biblical text as a whole in its final ("canonical") form, remaining sensitive to its literary merit, theological import, and compelling power as the word of God.

Recognizing the needs of contemporary students, many of whom come to theological studies as a second career with no previous biblical or even humanities training, this introduction responds to the demand for a clear, comprehensive presentation of pertinent issues and data, set forth succinctly and with helpful explanations of technical material.

T<small>HE</small> P<small>UBLISHERS</small>

CHAPTER 1

What Is the Pentateuch?

THE TERM "Pentateuch" is used by scholars to designate the first five books of the Old Testament (Genesis to Deuteronomy), which have been regarded since early times as the first of its three major divisions. The other two divisions are the Prophets (the "Former Prophets" — Joshua, Judges, Samuel, and Kings — and the "Latter Prophets" — Isaiah, Jeremiah, Ezekiel, and the "Book of the Twelve," the so-called Minor Prophets from Hosea to Malachi) and the Writings, comprising the other books.

The Pentateuch has always been an essential part of Holy Scripture, recognized as such by Jews and Christians alike. For the Jews, whose name for it is "the Torah," it holds the first and most authoritative place in their Scriptures, being traditionally regarded as the work of Moses. As the only person who spoke with God face to face (Exod. 33:11; Deut. 34:10), Moses was God's most authoritative spokesman, communicating the will of God to his people. For Christians also the Pentateuch is, together with the rest of the Old Testament, an essential part of the Holy Scriptures. In the Gospels, Jesus is represented as quoting or alluding to the authoritative teaching of "Moses" (i.e., the Pentateuch) more frequently than to any other Old Testament book; and references to it by the other New Testament writers are even more numerous.

In modern times some scholars have questioned the appropriateness of this traditional way of dividing the Old Testament books. It has been argued, on the one hand, that it is in the book of Joshua, with the account of Israel's settlement in the Promised Land, that the true conclusion of the Pentateuchal story is to be found. (These scholars speak of a "Hexateuch," meaning a group of six books.) Others contend that the real

1

conclusion of the story is to be found even later, with the history of the monarchy, in the books of Samuel or Kings. On the other hand, some scholars (e.g., Martin Noth) speak of a "Tetrateuch" (four books), on the grounds that Deuteronomy does not properly belong with the previous books but marks the beginning of another major historical work, the so-called Deuteronomistic History, comprising Deuteronomy, Joshua, Judges, Samuel, and Kings. Each of these proposals has merit. It is true that God's promise to Abraham that his descendants will possess and occupy the land of Canaan — a theme that in one way or another dominates the whole of the subsequent events — remains unfulfilled in the Pentateuchal narrative and only reaches its completion in Joshua. However, it is also a fact that Deuteronomy, which looks forward to the occupation of the land as the fulfillment of the original promise, makes an appropriate starting point for the events narrated in the books that follow. In addition, the language, style, and theological ideas of Deuteronomy have a greater affinity with those later books than with the preceding ones.

However, there are good reasons for retaining the notion of a Pentateuch and the traditional division of the text. The ancient title of "the Five Books of Moses," although unacceptable to modern scholarship as a statement about authorship, is not entirely inappropriate as a statement about the content of the story. Admittedly, the book of Genesis is entirely concerned with persons who lived and events that took place before Moses was born. However, the following four books are entirely dominated, from the human point of view, by the figure of Moses, whose birth is recorded at the very beginning of those books (Exod. 2:2) and his death at their very end (Deut. 34:5). That his death marked the "end of an era" is emphasized by a final passage (Deut. 34:10-12), which asserts the unique importance of the figure of Moses. The book of Joshua, which begins with a reference to Moses' death and proceeds immediately to the divine commissioning of his successor Joshua to lead the people into the land, clearly marks the start of an entirely new age. Later Judaism was to look back to Moses as the person who, under God, had not only laid the foundations of the subsequent life of Israel but furnished it so completely with its religious institutions that it needed nothing more to guide and sustain it as the uniquely chosen people of God. Viewed in this way, Genesis may be seen as an introduction to, or preparation for, that unique era.

2

The Contents of the Pentateuch

Genesis 1-11 (the so-called Primeval History) has a peculiar character of its own. It depicts a world in which the supernatural is commonplace — where God (and the "sons of God," Gen. 6:1-2) can converse and have relationships with human beings as a matter of course, and where snakes can have conversations with men and women. It begins with the creation of the world (heaven and earth) together with the heavenly bodies, the flora and fauna, and human beings, and then passes immediately to describe a series of human attempts to frustrate God's purpose for humanity and to claim for human beings powers and privileges which God had not intended them to have: the disobedience of the first man and woman (ch. 3), the destruction of a fellow human being (ch. 4); a semi-divine status (6:1-4). The total corruption of the human race with the exception of Noah leads God to determine its destruction (ch. 6). This is carried out by means of a devastating flood; but Noah and his family, together with representative specimens of the animal species, are saved by God's direction to build a boat (or "ark") on which they remain until the flood has subsided (chs. 7-8). So God plans, through Noah and his sons, to build a new humanity and a new human society. He promises never again to send such a flood on the earth to destroy the human race, establishing an "everlasting covenant" with it and giving the rainbow as a sign of this promise (ch. 9). But the Primeval History does not end on this hopeful note. On the contrary, ch. 11 recounts that a later generation once more attempted to defy God by building "a city and a tower with its top in the heavens" (the Tower of Babel), so making themselves as powerful as God himself (11:6). God responded by confusing the speech of the rebels so that they no longer understood one another, and scattering them over the face of the earth (11:6-9). This part of Genesis thus ends on a negative and menacing note which bodes ill for humanity's future well-being, as far as the narrative thread is concerned.

It is important to pay attention to the genealogical tables in these chapters (4:17-22; 5:1-32; 10:1-32; 11:10-29). One of the functions of these is to link the narratives together in a chronological series; but they also provide various kinds of additional information. Gen. 4:17-22 introduces the reader to those people who invented certain arts and ways of life beneficial to mankind; ch. 10 is an attempt to account for the origins and geographical locations of the nations of the world. More important for the structure and continuity of the Pentateuchal story is the genealogy

3

in 11:10-29, which gives the ancestry of Abram (Abraham in the later chapters). This introduces the significant statement with which this section of Genesis ends (11:31-32) that Abram's father Terah migrated with his family, including Abram and his wife Sarai (later Sarah) from Ur of the Chaldeans with the intention of going to the land of Canaan, but in fact settled in Haran. With this short narrative the link is made between the Primeval History and the main narratives of Genesis, the stories of the "patriarchs."

Genesis 12-50 is the story of a family. It concentrates on four generations of that family, first on three generations of individuals — father, son, and grandson — and then on the twelve sons of the head of the third generation, Jacob, who after wrestling with a mysterious adversary at the ford of the Jabbok, is renamed "Israel" (32:28). It is then clearly stated near the end of the book that Jacob's twelve sons "are the twelve tribes of Israel" (49:28). These chapters, then, take the story from the first mention of Abram in 11:26 to the first mention of Israel as a people, a people blessed by God with a special blessing. It is here that the subject of the Pentateuch first becomes clear: it is to be about Israel and about God's gracious nurture and protection of Israel in the remote past. The selective genealogies of chs. 1-11 have progressively narrowed down their scope and interest to one individual — Abram. Now the genealogy is widened out again to that of a larger group — the sons of Jacob/Israel and their families, the ancestors of what is to become a great nation.

Direct communication by God to individual persons, which we have seen to characterize chs. 1-11, continues with Abraham, Isaac, and Jacob. God's first words to Abraham, in which he commands him to leave Haran and proceed to an unknown destination, initiate a theme which recurs several times and dominates these "patriarchal" stories: the promise, in this case (12:1-3) that Abraham's descendants will become a great nation and that he will be especially blessed. In subsequent passages (especially 17:4-8; 22:17-18; 26:3-5, 24; 28:13-15; 35:10-12) the promise is repeated, first to Abraham himself and then to Isaac and Jacob, in somewhat different words, and with one notable addition: a promise of possession of the land of Canaan.

A further crucial theme which runs through these chapters is that of God's constant care in the protection of the lives of Abraham and his family from dangers and other circumstances which threaten them and so threaten the fulfillment of the promises. Twice Abraham and Sarah in their wanderings undertaken in obedience to God's initial command are

4

miraculously saved from the danger of death at the hands of foreign kings
— from Pharaoh (12:10-20) and from the king of Gerar (20:1-18) — and
materially rewarded instead. Isaac is similarly preserved (26:1-16). Sarah's
inability to bear children because of her advanced age is miraculously
overcome, with the result that Isaac, Abraham's heir, is born (17:15-19;
21:1-7). The life of Jacob, threatened by his brother Esau, is saved (ch.
27), and he is also preserved from other dangers (e.g., chs. 31, 33). Joseph
escapes from his brothers, who intend to kill him (ch. 37), and becomes
a great man in Egypt, second only to Pharaoh himself (41:37-45), and is
thus enabled to save his father and brothers from starvation (chs. 42-46).
The theme of divine providential care is put into words by Joseph himself
(45:7-8; 50:20), summing up the whole patriarchal story.

In the **book of Exodus** it is already a people rather than a family
whose fortunes are recounted, as indicated in Exod. 1:1-7. The expression
"sons of Israel" (Hebrew *beney yisrael*), which in v. 1 refers quite literally to
Jacob's sons — the individuals who entered Egypt with their families to
live there at Joseph's suggestion and at Pharaoh's invitation, seventy persons
all told — has already acquired in v. 7 the meaning "Israelites," which it
is to retain throughout Israel's history (so translated, e.g., in NRSV).

With Exod. 1:8 there begins a new era. Joseph is dead, and a new
pharaoh knows nothing about him. Pharaoh is, however, very aware of
Israel as a people, whose numbers have now become so great that they
constitute a threat to Egypt's security. The first chapters of Exodus recount
yet another threat to God's plan, this time on a massive scale: an attempt
to exterminate, or at least to enslave, an entire people (chs. 1-2). But again,
as in his previous dealings with the ancestors, God intervenes to save his
people from the danger which threatens them. The instrument chosen for
this purpose is Moses, who is himself destined with other male Israelite
babies to be killed at birth, but whose life is saved in an incident which
is ostensibly fortuitous (2:1-10). As God's emissary (chs. 3-4) the adult
Moses secures the release of the Israelites from Egypt by means of a
devastating series of plagues which demonstrate God's overwhelming
power (chs. 7-12), and they depart from Egypt.

Pharaoh's change of mind about letting the Israelites go (14:5) creates
a new danger: they are now pursued with hostile intent by the Egyptian
army. But again the threat is averted. The Israelites escape by means of a
miraculous crossing of the "sea" (Hebrew *yam suph*, probably "Sea of
Reeds") on dry land, while the pursuing Egyptian troops are drowned (ch.
14).

5

The Israelites' release from bondage in Egypt and the subsequent crossing of the "sea" are represented as the supreme demonstration of the power of the God of Israel as well as his love for Israel, and "the people feared the Lord and believed in the Lord and in his servant Moses." Yet the book of Exodus also introduces a quite different theme: Israel's constant ingratitude and lack of faith. This already appears in a reluctance to accept Moses as God's emissary (5:21), and then becomes a constant motif in the subsequent forty years' journey in the wilderness in search of the Promised Land (16:3ff.; 17:1-7; 32), continuing into the book of Numbers. More than once (e.g., Exod. 32:7-14) the continuation of the special relationship which God had established with Israel is endangered. Only when Moses pleads with God for the people's forgiveness is its continuance promised — but not without due punishment (32:31-35).

It is at Sinai, "the mountain of the Lord," that Israel encounters God and that he binds them with a covenant (Exod. 24) and they promise to obey his commands. These are expressed in the Ten Commandments (Exod. 20:1-17) which Moses brought down from the mountain, and in a longer series of laws which God conveys to the people through Moses (20:22–23:19). Israel remains at the mountain for a long time, and many further laws are added: Exod. 25-40, the whole of the book of Leviticus, and parts of the book of Numbers. Finally (Num. 10:33), the people of Israel set out from the mountain. The remainder of Numbers describes their further journeys and attempts, through many vicissitudes, still frustrated by further disobedience, to reach the Promised Land, having been condemned to remain in the wilderness for a whole generation — forty years (Num. 14:26-35). Even Moses is not permitted to enter the Promised Land on account of the people's sins (Num. 20:12; 27:13-14; Deut. 1:37, etc.).

The **book of Deuteronomy** consists almost entirely of words spoken by Moses (the longest of his speeches runs from 5:1 to 26:19 and includes an entire code of laws, chs. 12-26). The scene is the plain of Moab on the east side of the river Jordan; Israel is poised to cross the river and to take possession at last of the Promised Land on the other side. Unlike the other books of the Pentateuch, Deuteronomy begins with a recapitulation of past history. In his first speech (1:1–4:40), Moses reminds the people of the events that have taken place since their departure from Horeb (clearly identical with Sinai, although not called that here). The dominant notes of these chapters, as also of other parts of the book, are their homiletic character and an insistence on God's care for Israel in overcoming the

6

hostility of the nations on the east side of the Jordan and the conquest of territory there — the first of Israel's territorial conquests. Another prominent theme is the need to beware of the anger of a God who, though a loving God and the giver of all good gifts, is also a terrible God, to be feared.

A second speech (5:1–26:19) is also hortatory. The first part (5:1–11:32) includes a reminder of the promulgation of the Ten Commandments at Horeb/Sinai (5:6-21), recited in full for a second time. Here also is the famous "Shema": "Hear, O Israel: The Lord your God, the Lord is one [or "the Lord alone"]. You shall love the Lord your God with all your heart, and with all your soul, and with all your might" (6:4-5), later to be treasured by the Jews as expressing the essence of their faith. The Shema speaks of God's great gifts to Israel (including the Law given on Horeb/Sinai), but also of Israel's history of sin and God's forbearance, and Israel's unworthiness and inability to achieve anything for themselves. Prosperity is promised if they are faithful and obedient, but disobedience will bring on them curses rather than blessings.

The laws which follow (chs. 12-26) are referred to in 29:1 as "the words of the covenant that the Lord commanded Moses to make with the Israelites in the land of Moab, in addition to the covenant that he had made with them at Horeb." This second covenant was then executed (ch. 29), and its "words" — that is, the preceding code of laws — were written by Moses in a "book," the book of the law (31:24), which was to be a "witness" against the people if they disobeyed (vv. 26-29). The laws themselves are in part a repetition of the laws promulgated at Sinai according to Exod. 20:22–23:19, but many of them are expressed somewhat differently and in a somewhat different spirit, while others do not appear in Exodus at all. They begin with an important new requirement that Israel when it settles in Canaan shall no longer offer its sacrifices in a variety of places but only at an (unidentified) "place that the Lord will choose" (Deut. 12:13-14).

Deuteronomy ends with a number of shorter pericopes. There is a more detailed warning about the respective effects of future obedience and disobedience in terms of curses and blessings (chs. 27-28), including a warning that disobedience will lead to military defeat and captivity to a foreign nation and to exile from the land (28:25-44). Then follow the account of the making of the second covenant (ch. 29), Moses' farewell speech (ch. 31), the Song of Moses (ch. 32), and Moses' blessing of the tribes of Israel (ch. 33). In 32:48-52 Moses receives instructions concerning the place where he is to die; he will be able to see from the summit of Mount Nebo the land which God is to give to Israel, but is again told that he will not enter it himself. Deut. 34:1-8 records Moses' death. It is stated in 34:9 that Joshua, who had already been commissioned by God as Moses' successor (31:23), had also been consecrated by Moses for his task by the imposition of Moses' hands, and that the Israelites obeyed him, as God had commanded. Finally in 34:10-12 comes the assessment of Moses previously mentioned (p. 2).

In these final chapters, although the appointment of Joshua to lead the people into the Promised Land clearly looks to the future, there is an unmistakable sense of a definite ending, not found in any other book of the Pentateuch. The era of Moses, which began at the beginning of the book of Exodus, is at an end. It is made clear that this had been the decisive era for Israel, in which Israel had been rescued from bondage in Egypt and, at Sinai/Horeb, had received from God at the hands of Moses its definitive character as God's chosen people, furnished with everything necessary for its future life.

The Pentateuch as "Story"

The above outline is an attempt — necessarily somewhat selective — to present the main features of the "story line" of the Pentateuch as it would appear to someone reading it for the first time as a "book," unaware of critical notions of multiple authorship, sources, gradual growth over a long period of time, and the like. It is most important to read it in this way before beginning to study those other ways of reading it, in order to be able to answer the question which is the title of this chapter, "What is the Pentateuch?" as distinct from the question, "How did the Pentateuch become what it is?" This second question will be considered in the following chapters of this book. That there are minor inconsistencies in the story would no doubt occur to a perceptive reader. But unless he or she is a committed deconstructionist, these will not be enough to disturb an appreciation of the Pentateuch as "story." That is the way in which it has been read for many centuries by the great majority of both Jews and Christians.

The Pentateuch presents itself as a *history.* That is, it is a narrative or "story" in which the events which it narrates, from the creation of the world to the death of Moses, are arranged in chronological sequence. Even the recapitulation of past events in the early chapters of Deuteronomy is assigned its place in the narrative as part of a speech of Moses spoken at a later time; it is not represented as the composition of the narrator of the Pentateuch. Again, although about one-half of the text of the Pentateuch consists of laws rather than being a narrative of events, these are stated to have been promulgated by God or through Moses at particular moments, and so are formally part of the ongoing story. The same applies to the poems which occur from time to time in the text. They are stated to have been recited or sung by particular persons at particular moments in the course of the story. At every point the reader is told what happened and when. The impression given to the reader is thus of a grand sweep of history. It would be wrong to think of the Pentateuch as just a miscellaneous collection of stories, laws, and poems lacking an overall theme and purpose.

The *theme* of the Pentateuch is not difficult to discern. It is the story of the birth and adolescence of a nation. Such a work is not in itself unique in the literatures of the ancient world, particularly in the world of late antiquity, nor is the fact that it begins with an account of the origin of the world itself unique. Its notion of a benevolent deity presiding over the nation's destiny is not by any means unusual. However, in some crucial respects the Pentateuch is unique as a national history. This is true of its portrayal of the divine. The Pentateuch as it presents itself to the reader knows of one, supreme God. Although this God is known, especially in Genesis, by a variety of names — the Lord (Yahweh), the Lord God, God Almighty (El Shadday), God Most High (El Elohim), or simply as God (El or Elohim) — for the Pentateuch these are all names of the same God who is the creator of the world and supreme over it. There are no rival gods.

But equally unique is the portrayal of God's chosen people, Israel. The Pentateuch is no boastful, triumphalist work lauding Israel over all other nations for its virtues, its merits, or its valor. On the contrary, Israel is represented as constantly rebellious, ungrateful, disobedient to God. Yet it is also portrayed as completely without any ability to achieve anything by its own efforts, totally dependent on God for any successes it may have. The story of Israel in the Pentateuch is not one of which the nation can be proud. If it is to become a great nation (Gen. 12:2), this will be through no merit of its own. In contrast with other national histories, the Pentateuch does not present to its readers the picture of a glorious past.

In fact, it is God rather than Israel who has the leading role in the

Pentateuch. From the very beginning (Gen. 1-11) God's intentions and actions with regard to his human creatures are represented as just and severe, yet merciful. The first man and woman are expelled from the garden for disobedience, but their lives are preserved. Even the first murderer, though banished from the presence of God, is given a chance to live out his life. Corrupt humanity is drowned, yet a new beginning is made with Noah. The presumption of the builders of the Tower of Babel is punished by their being divided and scattered throughout the earth and deprived of their common language, but the human race is nevertheless permitted to survive and multiply.

With God's choice and commissioning of Abraham, the theme of divine gift, human shortcoming, and divine forbearance — seen first as concentrated upon the fortunes of a single family and then on the children of Israel grown into a nation — becomes a constant and consistent feature of the Pentateuchal story. The threefold promises of blessing, numerous progeny, and possession of the land dominate much of the story. Although the last of these remains largely unfulfilled, the other two promises still hold, despite massive and frequent disobedience both before and after the encounter with God at Sinai. In an important sense, therefore, the Pentateuch as a whole teaches a *moral and religious lesson* which the reader is intended to heed and to take at the same time as both an encouragement to his own generation to trust God's gracious purpose and a warning to live a life of obedience in the future. This lesson is taught most unmistakably in the final book, Deuteronomy; but it is implicit in all the previous books. In some parts of the story this religious and theological note is more evident than in others; the story of Gen. 2-3, for example, has always been recognized as a profound parable of the human condition.

Finally, it is important that the Pentateuch should be appreciated as an outstanding *literary achievement.* Some parts of it, of course, are justly famous as "Bible stories." Others, however, hardly qualify by themselves as literary masterpieces. But taken as a whole, the Pentateuch is a kind of epic on a massive scale. The unknown person — called by modern scholars the "final redactor" — who was responsible for its final shape has taken a mass of material, some of it rather unpromising, and forged it into a compelling "story." Like Homer and other ancient writers who also told heroic tales of the remote past, usually in poetry, the redactor has introduced us, in prose rather than poetry, into a "world" unfamiliar to us but which has its own logic and its own rules. How this was achieved, and what were the materials which he used will be the subject of the next chapter of this book.

For Further Reading

Alter, Robert, and Kermode, Frank, eds. *The Literary Guide to the Bible*. Cambridge, Mass.: Harvard University Press and London: Collins, 1987, 36-101.

Blenkinsopp, Joseph. *The Pentateuch: An Introduction to the First Five Books of the Bible*. New York: Doubleday and London: SCM, 1992, ch. 2.

Clines, David J. A. *The Theme of the Pentateuch*. JSOT Supplement 10. Sheffield: JSOT Press, 1978.

CHAPTER 2

Who Wrote It?
Problems of Composition

I T HAS LONG BEEN recognized that the traditional view — not stated in the Pentateuch itself, but already assumed elsewhere in the Old Testament — that Moses was the author of the Pentateuch cannot be correct. This conclusion was not derived from the fact that Moses' death and burial are recorded in the Pentateuch itself (Deut. 34:5-8). It would after all be possible to regard this final chapter, which also refers to the appointment of Joshua as Moses' successor and concludes with a general assessment of Moses' achievements, as simply a postscript added to a work (Genesis to Deuteronomy) which was, with this single exception, the work of Moses himself. This view was actually held in later Judaism. A passage in the Jewish Talmud attributes the verses in question to Joshua. The rejection of Mosaic authorship rests, as will be seen below, on other criteria.

It should perhaps be stressed at this point that, despite the vast amount of scholarly work which has been published — especially during the past century — concerning the authorship, date, and history of composition of the Pentateuch, these are basically side issues. The real interest for readers of the Bible does not lie here. If it did, the present generation of readers would experience only frustration. For although it may be true that recent scholars have succeeded in exposing many of the errors of earlier critics, it must be admitted that as far as assured results are concerned we are no nearer to certainty than when critical study of the Pentateuch began. There is at the present moment no consensus whatever about when, why, how, and through whom the Pentateuch reached its present form, and opinions about the dates of composition of its various parts differ by more

12

than five hundred years. This chapter, therefore, may be regarded by many as an irrelevancy as regards a serious understanding of the meaning and purpose of the Pentateuch, though the questions with which it is concerned remain — and are likely to remain — a major item on the agenda of academic Old Testament study. The important question is not one of the sources available to the compiler but what the Pentateuch was intended to mean in its present form.

Doubts about — and even denials of — Mosaic authorship were voiced sporadically over the centuries by individual writers both Jewish and Christian and (later) both Catholic and Protestant, some of whom proposed specific dates and events in Israel's history for the Pentateuch's composition or for parts of it. One of the most important of such scholars was the twelfth-century Jewish scholar Ibn Ezra, who (though in an allusive way in order to avoid hostile criticism) pointed to a number of passages in Genesis and Deuteronomy which could only be understood as written from a standpoint much later than that of Moses. Here was an early example of the historical-critical method which was to play a crucial part in later, especially nineteenth-century, critical discussion. The seventeenth-century French Catholic priest Richard Simon may also be mentioned here. He regarded the Pentateuch as a compilation of numerous written sources of different dates. But no comprehensive investigation of the composition of the Pentateuch as a whole had as yet been undertaken.

A significant pioneer in this respect was another Frenchman, the physician Jean Astruc, who in 1753 published a study of Genesis, which he claimed had been constructed out of earlier written "memoirs." Astruc did not, however, reject Mosaic authorship, or at least editorship. Rather, his purpose was to defend it: it was Moses himself who had made the compilation. A feature of particular importance in Astruc's analysis was the discovery of a difference of terminology in different passages. In particular, Astruc distinguished two documents which differ in the ways in which they refer to God: one calls him by the name Jehovah ("the Lord" in most English versions), the other by the word Elohim ("God"). This early source (or documentary) theory marked the beginning of what was to be the dominant method of Pentateuchal criticism in the nineteenth and early twentieth centuries. In 1953 the bicentenary of the publication of Astruc's book was celebrated in recognition of his importance as the real initiator of modern Pentateuchal criticism. (See Roland de Vaux's paper read at the international Old Testament congress held at Copenhagen and subsequently published in VTS 1 [1953]: 182-198.)

Johann Gottfried Eichhorn in his introduction to the Old Testament (1780-1783) took up and developed Astruc's approach. He pointed to further stylistic distinctions between the two sources (or "strands") in Genesis, the "Yahwistic" and the "Elohistic" (subsequently dubbed "J," from the German spelling Jahve, and "E," respectively). A further refinement to the theory was made by Karl David Ilgen, who in 1798 anticipated later critical study by arguing that there are in fact not one but two distinct Elohistic sources, so making three sources in all.

Meanwhile two quite different approaches to the problem began to be pursued, leading to the development of the so-called fragment and supplement theories. In order to understand the rationale of these theories it may be useful to consider the general question of the main ways in which a literary work which is composite in character — that is, one which was not created in a single act of composition, but developed gradually over a period of years — may have reached its final form. First, the work may be the result of the combination of two or more older complete written works (the "documentary" method). Second, it may be the result of the combination of a number of isolated shorter units either written or oral (the "fragment" method). Third, it may have come about by the gradual expansion or supplementation of an original single work by additional material with the intention of modifying its character or extending its scope (the "supplement" method). In the case of a lengthy and complex work such as the Pentateuch, these three approaches are not necessarily mutually exclusive. One method may have been employed by a redactor in one part, another by a different redactor in another. For example, the formation of the legal parts of the Pentateuch may have occurred in a way quite different from the way in which narratives were combined.

The Fragment Hypothesis (dealing now not only with Genesis but with the whole Pentateuch) was espoused by another Catholic priest, Alexander Geddes (1792 and 1800), and by Johann Severin Vater (1802-1805). Vater postulated a series of unrelated fragmentary sources which continued to be accumulated over the years, resulting eventually in the completed Pentateuch at the time of the Babylonian Exile in the sixth century B.C. A weakness of this theory if applied wholesale to the Pentateuch is that if fails to identify a credible motive for the process. W. M. L. de Wette (1806, 1807) supported the Fragment Hypothesis, but only in part. He found it necessary to combine it with the Documentary Hypothesis. But de Wette also put forward a quite novel theory which was to become one of the principal bases of all subsequent Pentateuchal criti-

14

cism until recent years. Comparing the details of King Josiah of Judah's late seventh-century reform of the Jerusalem cult as described in 2 Kgs. 22-23 (and in another version in 2 Chr. 34-35) with the book of Deuteronomy, he argued that this reform was based on the laws of Deuteronomy, which must therefore be identical with the "book of the law" found in the temple and used to initiate the reform. On the assumption that that "book" was a recent composition, this thesis — which was widely, and eventually almost unanimously, accepted — was a breakthrough in Pentateuchal study, in that now for the first time a substantial part of the Pentateuch could be precisely dated.

This dating of Deuteronomy was to become the cornerstone of the "new documentary hypothesis" generally associated with the name of Julius Wellhausen, but which owed much to his predecessors, especially Eduard Reuss, Hermann Hupfeld, Abraham Kuenen, and Karl Heinrich Graf. It now became possible to attempt the dating of the other Pentateuchal sources J, E, and the "second Elohist," later known as P. Since they reflected earlier stages of the Israelite religion, J, E, and P were all at first thought to have preceded D (Deuteronomy) in point of time. Doubts, however, came to be expressed about the early dating of P, and it was Graf (1866) who finally established that the laws of P (in Leviticus and the latter part of Exodus) belong to the latest strand in the Pentateuch, and that P is consequently its latest source, later than D. The four sources had been combined by a series of redactors, referred to as R^{JE}, R^D and R^P, whose participation in the process of composition, however, is never very clearly defined.

The Supplement Hypothesis, according to which the Pentateuch consists of a single basic source subsequently supplemented by later writing, had a number of advocates during the nineteenth century, including Friedrich Bleek, de Wette (toward the end of his life), and Franz Delitzsch. Some of its advocates, however, later abandoned this hypothesis. And although it has recently been revived in a somewhat different form, the future clearly lay with the Documentary Hypothesis.

The Documentary Hypothesis in its new form, finally presented in masterly fashion by Wellhausen in a series of publications from 1876 to 1884, dominated Pentateuchal study for almost a century. It was admittedly, and not surprisingly, vigorously opposed by conservative scholars such as Ernst Wilhelm Hengstenberg in Germany (in the earlier stages of the hypothesis) and Edward B. Pusey in England, who were fundamentally opposed to all biblical criticism, and by Catholic scholars. But in academic

15

circles in general, the Documentary Hypothesis came to be regarded as unassailable. Until very recent times it has been taken for granted by biblical scholars, who have treated its hypothetical sources or "documents" as though they actually existed as independent *books* providing reliable information about particular definable stages in the history of the religion of Israel.

As has already been suggested, Wellhausen was a historian, concerned not only with a literary question but with the history of Israel and more particularly with the history of its religion. He saw the sources or "strata" *(Schichten)* of the Pentateuch as reflecting different stages of this historical development, especially of the development of the cult. Although he recognized E as a distinct source (though one which was often difficult to distinguish from J — the criterion of the two divine names is only applicable to Genesis and the first few chapters of Exodus; after that this distinction breaks down), Wellhausen worked mainly with three strata, the "Jehovist" (a combination of J and E), D, and P. He argued that both JE and the stories in Judges, Samuel, and Kings (before their later editing) present a picture of Israel and its worship which is clearly earlier than that presented by D and P, and indeed earlier than the time of the eighth-century prophets. He further contended that the influence of those prophets is discernible in D, however, while the elaborate system of laws in P (which is presupposed in the books of Chronicles) is postexilic and represents a degeneration from the spirit of the great prophets. Also, JE belongs to the early part of the period of the monarchy, before the eighth century. (It is precisely this notion, that Israel at such an early stage of cultural development could have been the first people ever to conceive and produce such extensive "historical" works, that is one of the main drawbacks to the hypothesis.)

It is unnecessary here to pursue the later history of the new Documentary Hypothesis in detail. One of its notable features was the further multiplication of sources. Attempts were made to distinguish E more clearly from J. J itself was, on the basis of supposed linguistic and theological distinctions, separated into two sources, J^1 and J^2, and even into three (Otto Eissfeldt proposed a "lay source" L, Robert H. Pfeiffer an Edomite or "southern" source S, Georg Fohrer a "nomadic" source N), and E also into E^1 and E^2. A distinct "Holiness Code" (Lev. 17-26) was "discovered" embedded in P, and P itself was fragmented into several successive strands. This process of dissection was to a large extent based on an unrealistic notion that authors are always completely consistent, so that differences in statements of fact, point of view, or language infallibly indicate the work of different authors. In some cases too the supposed inconsistencies are minute, too inconsiderable to be significant.

This kind of criticism, though hardly recognized at the time, represented a partial disintegration of the Documentary Hypothesis and a tendency toward a revival of the Fragment Hypothesis. It also served to raise questions, hardly before considered, about the nature of the supposed sources: were they unitary works, or were they themselves collections of heterogeneous material?

It was a younger contemporary of Wellhausen, Hermann Gunkel, who addressed himself to questions of this kind in relation to the book of Genesis. In his commentary on that book (first edition, 1901), he attempted to go back behind J and E to discover how its various stories had originated and taken shape in an earlier, preliterary period. Gunkel made use of the investigation of European folklore that had begun in the late eighteenth century and had been further developed in the early nineteenth century by Jacob and Wilhelm Grimm; he especially employed the work of his own contemporary, the Danish folklorist Axel Olrik on the early Icelandic *Sagen* or traditional, orally transmitted, tales of the preliterary past. Following a set of "epic laws" enunciated by Olrik, Gunkel classified the stories of Genesis (which he believed to have originated independently of one another) according to their formal characteristics with a view to uncovering the various situations in which they had arisen. In this, he was the pioneer of the method of "form criticism." In the third edition of his commentary Gunkel stated clearly that "Genesis is a collection of *Sagen*," which had originated at an early stage in Israel's history and had been handed down orally over a long period of time before being committed to writing.

Gunkel was thus not only the first "form critic"; he was also the first "tradition critic." He did not abandon the Documentary Hypothesis. Rather, Gunkel attempted to trace the gradual combination of the individual stories — especially those concerning the patriarchs Abraham and Jacob — into "circles of *Sagen*" and their eventual collection in written form by the authors of J and E. This "history of traditions" method was subsequently extended and applied to the whole narrative tradition of the Pentateuch by other scholars, notably Hugo Gressmann.

Gerhard von Rad (1938) built upon Gunkel's work on the oral tradition and used it as a foundation for a comprehensive theory of the development of the Pentateuchal traditions. He held that the main themes

17

of those traditions — the entry into Egypt of Israel's ancestors, their oppression in Egypt, their deliverance in the Exodus, their guidance to their final destination, and the gift of the land of Canaan — were brought together to become the "common heritage" of all the tribes at the celebration of the Feast of Weeks held at Gilgal in the time of the Judges. The evidence for this he found in a number of biblical passages, most clearly in Deut. 26:5-9, which he called a "Little Credo," recited at the annual offering of the firstfruits and containing all these elements in a liturgical prayer. The only main element of tradition lacking was the giving of the Law at Sinai; this was an entirely separate tradition celebrated at the Feast of Tabernacles at Shechem. The two sets of tradition were expanded and continued to develop separately until they were combined and committed to writing by the Yahwist (J), a designation which for von Rad seems to represent the entire pre-Deuteronomistic narrative tradition, including the older parts of Gen. 1-11, which the Yahwist was himself responsible for incorporating.

Von Rad's dating of the Yahwist is even earlier than that proposed by Wellhausen: the reign of Solomon (tenth century), the age of Israel's imperial expansion. This dating was connected with von Rad's view that at that time Israel — or its ruling class — experienced a strong cultural impulse, the consequence of international contacts especially with the superior culture of Egypt, resulting in an unusually swift development of literary as well as other skills (the so-called Solomonic enlightenment). The Yahwist's history and other narrative works were a product of this cultural revolution; and in an age of political confidence this history not unnaturally took the form of an account of the origins of the nation, which was now for the first time enabled to take pride in its past.

The influence of von Rad's work was at first immense. However, both his notion of a "Solomonic enlightenment" and his theory of the "Little Credo" have now lost much of their credibility. The former is now regarded as greatly exaggerated, partly because historical writing comparable with von Rad's Yahwist's history was not an art practiced in Egypt, while the Credo in Deut. 26:5-9 (which is part of the Deuteronomic laws) and similar passages are now believed to have been composed at a much later date, being late summaries of the earlier traditions rather than the starting point of their development.

Martin Noth's *A History of Pentateuchal Traditions* (1948) is in many respects a continuation of the work of von Rad. It is a much larger work than that of von Rad, and attempts to describe the entire process of the compilation of the Pentateuch (though in fact Noth concerned himself here only with the first four books — the "Tetrateuch," excluding Deuteronomy) "from beginning to end" in all its details. Each of the "themes" of von Rad's "Little Credo" was originally a separate tradition, the property of a particular tribe or group of tribes preserving its own recollection of its past experiences. These were pooled when the tribes united to form the tribal league or "amphictyony" which constituted the earliest Israel, and became the common tradition of the whole nation. This single narrative, which may or may not have been a written work, Noth called G (for *Grundlage*, "foundation"). The later J and E, which *were* written works, were separate histories which drew on the common material of G but added new material of their own. Eventually they were combined, E being preserved only in a partial form as a series of "enrichments" of the henceforth dominant J. Another prominent feature of Noth's work was his skepticism about the historicity of the stories about Moses. He did not doubt the actual existence of Moses, but believed that hardly any authentic material had been preserved about him.

Noth's reconstruction of the formation of the Pentateuch seemed at first very impressive. Comparatively few of his theses, however, have survived unscathed. His postulation of G has met with little acceptance; and his notion of an "amphictyony" is now completely discredited as is also, in many circles, his radical skepticism about the figure of Moses. Many of his particular arguments about the combination of specific traditions have been dismissed as unduly speculative and lacking in proof. Most of all, however, Noth's views about oral traditions have been severely questioned.

Thus Gunkel, von Rad, and Noth all retained the Documentary Hypothesis in their own ways. It was on their views about the gradual development of orally transmitted traditions before their committal to writing that they principally differed from Wellhausen. Subsequent study by anthropologists of the traditions of modern preliterate peoples has, however, revealed that the notion that such traditions can be orally preserved over many generations is a false one. After two or three generations these traditions tend to become so seriously distorted as to be unrecognizable or to disappear altogether. This fact has led to a growing tendency to reject the idea that the stories concerning such figures as Abraham, Jacob, and Moses can be much older than the written sources. Together with this, there is a growing tendency to doubt the antiquity of the written sources themselves, and to suggest that very little of the Pentateuch is older then the sixth century B.C. or even later. Nevertheless, the Documentary Hypothesis continues to be accepted by some scholars (see below).

The Swedish scholar Ivan Engnell, whose early death in 1964 left his work uncompleted and many of his ideas unpublished, was a thorough-going advocate of the tradition-historical method. He completely rejected the existence of the sources postulated by the Documentary Hypothesis. Together with other Swedish scholars, he held a strong belief in the reliability of the transmission of oral traditions, and, although convinced that the Pentateuch is to all intents and purposes a postexilic work, he held that its narratives had been transmitted orally over a period of many centuries. Engnell thus succeeded in combining a theory of late written composition with a belief in the antiquity of much of the material which it contains. This ancient material was finally edited by P in what Engnell called the "P work," distinguishing this from the "D work" of Deuter-onomy and the following "historical" books. Engnell's theories have received comparatively little subsequent attention, no doubt partly because he did not live to expound them fully.

Ever since the rediscovery of the Egyptian and Mesopotamian civi-lizations in the nineteenth century, attempts have been made to relate the Pentateuchal data to this international background — a matter of obvious importance for determining the antiquity of the Pentateuchal narratives and laws. Here it is possible only to refer to two of these investigations.

A matter of perennial debate has been the dating of what came to be known as the "patriarchal age," in other words, the attempt to discover what period of ancient Near Eastern history best fits the stories of Abraham and his family. Several possibilities in the second millennium B.C. were discussed by historians, archaeologists, and biblical scholars. One theory which for a time attracted particular attention associated the patriarchal stories with data provided by a collection of family archives from the Mesopotamian city of Nuzi, dating from the fifteenth and fourteenth centuries B.C. and mainly published from the 1920s on. Analogies were drawn between certain prac-tices of the patriarchs not attested in the Old Testament outside Genesis and certain family and legal customs at Nuzi which appeared to be peculiar to the Hurrian-speaking peoples of these texts. Subsequent improved knowl-edge both of Hurrian and of other Mesopotamian legal and family customs has, however, revealed that these practices have either been misunderstood or were in fact not confined either to Nuzi or to the second millennium, but are also attested more generally and in the first millennium as well. Thomas L. Thompson in *The Historicity of the Patriarchal Narratives* (1974), whose conclusions have been confirmed by other scholars, showed that not only the Nuzi hypothesis but also other attempts to locate the patriarchal age in history were without substance and that there is in fact no way of demonstrating the antiquity of the patriarchal stories of Genesis. John Van Seters (*Abraham in History and Tradition,* 1975) and others have argued with some plausibility that these reflect rather the concerns of the middle of the first millennium or even later. The search for the "historical Moses" has been no more successful.

A second theory based on Near Eastern parallels was put forward in 1954 by George E. Mendenhall. This was concerned not with Genesis but with the idea of a covenant (Hebrew *berith*) between Yahweh and Israel found especially in the Exodus accounts of the covenant at Sinai (which were generally supposed to be early) and with the Pentateuchal laws which were considered as constituting the conditions of obedience then imposed by Yahweh on Israel. Mendenhall linked this notion of a divinely imposed covenant both in contents and form with extant Hittite treaties imposed by human suzerains on their vassals, dating from the fourteenth and thirteenth centuries, suggesting that it was on a generally current familiarity with that kind of treaty that the concept of a *divine* covenant with Israel was based. This theory was more fully developed by Klaus Baltzer (1971).

However, like the Nuzi hypothesis, this theory, although at first widely accepted, was destined to have only a temporary success. It was pointed out on the basis of later discoveries that the international treaty form continued to be in use during the first millennium, many centuries later than the Hittite treaties, and that if Israel did in fact borrow the notion from elsewhere this borrowing could have taken place as late as the seventh century B.C. In 1969 Lothar Perlitt argued that not only the treaty form but the very idea of a covenant between Yahweh and Israel was an invention of the Deuteronomists and thus could not be earlier than the seventh century. This late date for the covenant idea continues to be disputed; but the theory of a direct analogy with Hittite treaties made in the time of Moses is no longer regarded as plausible.

The tendency to regard the Pentateuch as essentially a late composition was strongly reinforced by Van Seters, who retained the term Yahwist (J) but, while leaving the question of date theoretically open, offered evidence which suggested that it best fits the late monarchic or exilic period. Of the stories of Abraham and his family he wrote: "There is nothing in this presentation of the 'nomadic' patriarchs which is inappropriate to the portrayal of pastoral life in the period of the late Judean monarchy or exilic periods, but there is much that speaks against the choice of any earlier period" (p. 38). Thus, while he retained the notion of written "sources," Van Seters abandoned the Wellhausian scheme of successive "histories" stretching over a period of several centuries. Hans Heinrich Schmid, writing about "The So-Called Yahwist" (1976), expressed somewhat similar views, though for him the Pentateuch is a work closely associated with the Deuteronomists, who were also responsible for the "Deuteronomistic History" (Joshua, Judges, Samuel, Kings), so recounting the entire "history" from the creation of the world to the fall of the Judean monarchy in the early sixth century.

Rolf Rendtorff in *The Problem of the Process of Transmission in the Pentateuch* (1977; English translation, 1990) discussed traditional source criticism and tradition history as methods of approaching the question of composition. He saw the two as totally incompatible, arguing that it was a mistaken loyalty to source criticism which had prevented such scholars as von Rad and Noth from carrying their tradition-historical work to its proper conclusion. Like Schmid, Rendtorff regarded the Pentateuch as basically a Deuteronomistic composition. While virtually all earlier scholars had left room for P as an independent continuous source, Rendtorff regarded the "priestly" contribution as limited in scope and lacking in homogeneity. (More will be said about D and P later in this chapter.) Rendtorff's method was to begin by considering the smallest elements of tradition and, abandoning the notion of continuous sources, to endeavor to show how these had been built up through stages first into intermediate complexes and finally into larger blocks of material each with its own theme. These larger blocks (e.g., the Exodus story) had remained entirely independent of one another until they were combined at a late stage to form a comprehensive "history."

Rendtorff's pupil Erhard Blum in two works on the composition of the patriarchal stories (1984) and of the Pentateuch as a whole (1990) developed Rendtorff's work further, tracing the process of composition in greater detail than Rendtorff had thought possible. He also assigned a greater role to the work of individual authors of complexes of intermediate size such as the Jacob-Laban stories. Blum was particularly skeptical about the possibility that the traditions originated at a time before the period of the monarchy. In his second book he saw the priestly material as an attempt to correct certain elements of the Deuteronomistic theology; the Pentateuch is then a postexilic compromise between two schools of thought, made under the impulse of the Persian demand for a "Jewish law."

This chapter has so far been concerned mainly with the material which has for many years been known as the work of the Yahwist (J) and which has been generally at the center of the debate. But what of the remaining material, known to the Documentary Hypothesis under the symbols E, D, and P?

As has already been seen, the Elohist has always been a somewhat shadowy figure, in that even those most committed to the "four-document theory" found it difficult to distinguish E from J, especially outside Genesis. The strongest evidence for a parallel source to J was probably the existence of what were taken to be duplicate accounts of identical events found in different chapters (e.g., the expulsion of Hagar and Ishmael, Gen. 16 and 21) and passages in which it appeared that two accounts had been woven together, causing internal duplication of details (e.g., the story of the Flood, Gen. 6-9, and parts of the story of Joseph, notably Gen. 37). Differences of point of view (theology) and to some extent of language were taken to indicate the existence of a separate continuous source (E) rather than of a number of fragmentary additions, though it was admitted that E had been only partly preserved, having been inserted into the now more continuous J narrative.

In 1933 Paul Volz and Wilhelm Rudolph made a detailed study of the supposed E source in Genesis, concluding that there was no evidence for its existence: the passages in question could be adequately accounted for in a variety of other ways. In 1938 Rudolph extended this investigation to include the remainder of the Pentateuch (and also the book of Joshua, to which also the Documentary Hypothesis was commonly applied). This theory caused something of a scandal in Old Testament scholarship, and gained little acceptance at the time. However, despite attempts such as that of Hans Walter Wolff (1972) to rehabilitate the Elohist as a distinct source with its own theological point of view, it has ceased to be a significant element in Pentateuchal research. Modern approaches to Old Testament narratives based on contemporary literary theory, such as that of Robert Alter's *The Art of Biblical Narrative* (1981), have shown that duplications in narratives — which are by no means absent from modern fiction! — may be explained as a deliberate feature of literary technique employed by single authors for purposes of emphasis and to give artistic structure to their works.

The book of Deuteronomy raises distinct questions of its own, which will be discussed in chapter 6 below. Although the dating of the Code of Deuteronomy (Deut. 12-26) to the time of Josiah in the seventh century was a cornerstone on which the chronological succession of all four sources of the Pentateuch according to the Documentary Hypothesis was based, D was believed until very recently to be a source quite distinct from the other three, of which virtually no traces were to be found in the other four books. But this view has now been challenged. Both Schmid (1976) and Rendtorff (1977, 1983) have pointed to evidence of Deuteronomic theology in Genesis-Numbers. Rendtorff spoke of a redaction or reworking of the whole Pentateuch which "in its ideas and language is closely related to Deuteronomy" (*The Problem of the Process of Transmission in the Pentateuch*, 99). He also argued that this was the final redaction, so rejecting the general view that it is P which is the latest strand in the Pentateuch (see below).

Schmid, writing after Rendtorff's 1975 article on the question, differs from him in that he retains the concept of a Yahwist but dates this work (with Van Seters) after the conclusion of the monarchic period. He sees it as a complex literary and theological work rather than as the work of a single author, which "belongs in the proximity of the Deuteronomic-Deuteronomistic . . . tradition-forming and literary work." Schmid, however, does not define the relationship between this "Yahwist" and this "Deuteronomist" more closely. He does not deal with the question of P. Whatever may be the final judgment on the general views of Schmid and Rendtorff, their views about some kind of "Deuteronomic" influence on Genesis-Numbers constitute a new development which will certainly need to be taken into account in future Pentateuchal study.

The bulk of the material attributed to P consists of laws mainly concerned with the details of sacrificial worship and with the appointment and functions of the priesthood. But there are also a number of narratives associated with it, including the creation story in Gen. 1 and various incidents connected with the leadership of Moses, scattered throughout the books from Genesis to Numbers. The view that P is the latest strand in the Pentateuch dates from the recognition that there are two "Elohistic" strands in the Pentateuch, first proposed by Graf in 1866 (see above). This view was generally accepted until recently. The main points which remained in dispute were as follows:

1. The date of P (exilic or postexilic?).
2. The question whether P is not only the final strand, but also constitutes the final *redaction* of the Pentateuch: in other words, whether it was the author(s) of P who created the Pentateuch in its final form,

incorporating all the earlier material, or whether the final act of composition was the work of a later, final redactor who put together all four strands to make the completed work.

3. Whether the author(s) of P incorporated earlier, preexilic priestly lore or were interested only in presenting a new legislation solely concerned with the practice of their own time — or, if they worked during the Exile, with what they intended should become actual practice (compare the anticipatory legislation of Ezek. 40-48).

4. Whether the legislation of P is homogeneous or whether it contains a series of supplements to an original core reflecting a need for modification of the original.

5. The relationship between the narrative and the legal parts of P.

The legislation of P, or of the material commonly attributed to P, will be considered in chapter 7 below. The relative consensus regarding P as a whole has been challenged in recent years. As already stated, for Rendtorff P is *not* the final strand of the Pentateuch, and indeed is not a continuous source at all. He has argued, partly but not wholly on the grounds of style, that P's supposed narratives are not genuine narratives, but are rather theological interpretations of other material. Further, although P contains a series of brief chronological notices scattered throughout the Pentateuch, these lack homogeneity of style. They do not, as has been supposed, constitute a framework for the narrative corpus, but are merely sporadic. In short, P is not a connected narrative source — a point made already in 1933 by Volz in an appendix to his and Rudolph's work, entitled "P is no narrator"!

The conventional view of an exilic or postexilic date for P has now also been challenged by two Israeli scholars, Menahem Haran (1978, 1981) and Avi Hurvitz (1982), and by the American scholar Jacob Milgrom (1991). These reject the view that P's legislation reflects the cultic practice of the postexilic temple. Haran connects this legislation with the cultic reform carried out by Hezekiah. Hurvitz has carried out a thorough investigation of its language and style, especially comparing it with the laws of Ezekiel, and has concluded that it precedes Ezekiel rather than postdates it, as had been generally supposed. Thus P, like the other "sources" of the Pentateuch, has been thrown back into the melting pot.

The existence of P as a Pentateuchal source is the main aspect of the Documentary Hypothesis retained by Van Seters. This scholar remains a "documentary" critic in as far as he still speaks of a Yahwist. But for him the Yahwist is a late writer who is virtually the author of the Pentateuch, a historian who out of a mass of both early and contemporary traditions composed a history of the origins of the nation — to which, however, a later P made some further contributions. (However, if P is to be dated earlier [Haran and Hurvitz], the Pentateuch in its final form may be to all intents and purposes the work of a single writer.) Van Seters's main contribution to the debate is his conception of the Pentateuch as the work of a *historian.*

Earlier views of J or JE as preexilic and the work of "the world's first historian" suffered from the improbability that Israel alone at such an early date should have been capable of conceiving and producing a work covering such an extensive period and manifesting such a highly developed concept of historical purpose and of causation when the far more culturally advanced civilizations of Egypt and Mesopotamia were apparently incapable of doing so. Van Seters, by moving the "Yahwist" down the centuries, brought this achievement within the chronological range of the earliest Greek historians of the sixth and fifth centuries B.C., notably Herodotus, who did in fact achieve works of this kind. Without stressing any possible direct relationship between the Pentateuch and these Greek historians, Van Seters demonstrated that the Pentateuch strikingly resembles the Greek authors in various ways, both in style and also in its aims. The Pentateuch was an attempt to give the Jewish nation, in a late stage of its history, a sense of identity and of its past. In my *The Making of the Pentateuch* (1987) I have attempted to support Van Seters's thesis, while further suggesting that the hypothesis of a priestly author later than the (late) Yahwist may be unnecessary, and that the Pentateuch may be regarded as to all intents and purposes the work of a single author.

Readers previously unacquainted with the problem of the composition of the Pentateuch will no doubt find the above historical outline of conflicting theories — sketchy and incomplete though it is — bewildering. But at least it will be clear, as stated at the beginning of this chapter, that although certain tendencies can perhaps be discerned — one of these may well be the use of literary theory to reveal more clearly the character of the completed Pentateuch as a *work of literature* — no unanimity about its provenance exists at the present time. The debate is likely to continue indefinitely, and whether a new consensus will eventually emerge is far from certain. It would therefore be premature to attempt either an assessment of the present situation or a prognostication of the future. But it is important to realize that in such a matter as this we are dealing entirely with hypotheses and not with facts. Proof, either in the mathematical or in the logical meaning of that word, will never be attainable. The only *fact* available to us is the text of the Pentateuch itself in all its complexity.

For Further Reading

Alter, Robert. *The Art of Biblical Narrative*. New York: Basic Books and London: Allen and Unwin, 1981.

Blenkinsopp, Joseph. *The Pentateuch: An Introduction to the First Five Books of the Bible*. New York: Doubleday and London: SCM, 1992, ch. 1.

Childs, Brevard S. *Introduction to the Old Testament as Scripture*. Philadelphia: Fortress and London: SCM, 1979, 112-135.

Driver, Samuel R. *Introduction to the Literature of the Old Testament*. 8th ed. Edinburgh: T. & T. Clark, 1909.

Eissfeldt, Otto. *The Old Testament: An Introduction*. New York: Harper and Oxford: Blackwell, 1965, 158-182. (First published in German, 1934; this translation is based on the 3rd German ed., 1964.)

Gunkel, Hermann. *The Legends of Genesis*. New York: Schocken, 1964. (Translated from the introduction to his first [German] commentary on Genesis, 1901.)

Haran, Menahem. "Behind the Scenes of History: Determining the Date of the Priestly Source," *JBL* 100 (1981): 321-333.

Hurvitz, Avi. *A Linguistic Study of the Relationship Between the Priestly Source and the Book of Ezekiel*. Paris: Gabalda, 1982.

Kaiser, Otto. *Introduction to the Old Testament*. Minneapolis: Augsburg and Oxford: Blackwell, 1975, 33-45. (First published in German, 1969.)

Mendenhall, George E. "Covenant Forms in Israelite Tradition," *BA* 17 (1954): 50-76. Repr. in *The BA Reader* 3, ed. E. F. Campbell, Jr., and David Noel Freedman. Garden City: Doubleday, 1970, 25-53.

Noth, Martin. *A History of Pentateuchal Traditions*. Englewood Cliffs, N.J.: Prentice-Hall, 1972. Repr. Atlanta: Scholars Press, 1989. (First published in German, 1948.)

von Rad, Gerhard. "The Form-Critical Problem of the Hexateuch," in *The Problem of the Hexateuch and Other Essays*. Edinburgh: Oliver & Boyd, 1966, 1-78. Repr. Philadelphia: Fortress and London: SCM, 1984. (First published in German, 1938.)

Rendtorff, Rolf. *The Old Testament: An Introduction*. London: SCM, 1985, and Philadelphia: Fortress, 1986, 131-164. (First published in German, 1983.)

————. *The Problem of the Process of Transmission in the Pentateuch.* JSOT Supplement 89. Sheffield: JSOT Press, 1990. (First published in German, 1977.)

Schmidt, Werner H. *Old Testament Introduction.* London: SCM, 1984, 44-61. (Translated from the 2nd German ed., 1982.)

Soggin, J. Alberto. *Introduction to the Old Testament.* OTL. Rev. ed. Philadelphia: Westminster and London: SCM, 1980, 83-98. (Translated from the Italian ed., 1974.)

Thompson, Thomas L. *The Historicity of the Patriarchal Narratives.* BZAW 133. Berlin: de Gruyter, 1974.

Van Seters, John. *Abraham in History and Tradition.* New Haven: Yale University Press, 1975.

————. *In Search of History: Historiography in the Ancient World and the Origins of Biblical History.* New Haven: Yale University Press, 1983.

Wellhausen, Julius. *Prolegomena to the History of Ancient Israel.* Edinburgh: A. & C. Black, 1885. Repr. Magnolia, Mass.: Peter Smith, 1977. (First published in German, 1878.)

Whybray, R. Norman. *The Making of the Pentateuch.* JSOT Supplement 53. Sheffield: JSOT Press, 1987.

Wolff, Hans Walter. "The Elohistic Fragments in the Pentateuch," *Interpretation* 26 (1972): 158-173.

See also Rolf Rendtorff, "The 'Yahwist' as Theologian? The Dilemma of Pentateuchal Criticism," with responses and reviews by various scholars in *JSOT* 3 (1977): 2-60.

CHAPTER 3

The "Primeval History" (Genesis 1-11)

THESE CHAPTERS must be regarded as a "prologue" to the Pentateuch rather than as part of the main body of the work. If the aim of the Pentateuch as a whole is to narrate a connected human "history" (even though in a sense different from that of modern historians), these chapters — which begin with the action of God even before the universe existed (Gen. 1:1-2) — can obviously not be based on any record of what actually "occurred." And although the later parts of these chapters refer to many names of human persons and in some cases (Cain, Abel, Enoch, Noah) recount their actions and even mention the number of years that they lived (ch. 5; 9:29; 11:10-32), the very longevity of these persons alone is enough to show that we are here dealing with a very different "world" even from that of the chapters which follow in Genesis — the stories about Abraham and his family.

These stories do not constitute a single narrative sequence. They have been linked together only in a very artificial way with long genealogies (4:17-22; 5:1-32; 10:1-32; 11:10-32). They are, in fact, "universal" stories. They deal not with human beings as we know them but with "giants" or "heroes" in something like the legendary sense of those words. They tell us how their authors, or their authors' contemporaries, imagined that it "might all have begun." However, as we shall see, they also had a much deeper purpose than that.

Many peoples have, or have had at some stage of their development, comparable stories about the origins of the world and the early history of the human race. Moreover, many of the stories in Gen. 1-11 have a "family" likeness to various "origin stories" current in the ancient Near Eastern milieu to which ancient Israel belonged (see *ANET,* 3-155, and the works listed at the end of this chapter). These all bear the marks of the particular civilizations — Egyptian, Mesopotamian, Hittite, etc. — which produced them, and Gen. 1-11 is no exception. The most obvious difference between the Israelite "universal history" and the others is that the Israelite stories — in their present form at least — are monotheistic. All the others are polytheistic. That is, only in the Israelite stories is all the divine action, from the creation of the world on, attributed to the unaided work of a single supreme God. Indeed, there is not the slightest suggestion that there are other gods, while in the non-Israelite stories there is a multitude of "gods." These ancient Near Eastern deities sometimes collaborate as a kind of "committee" but at other times violently or subtly oppose one another; none possesses universal power, though one may be more powerful than the others. The term "myth" is often applied to these stories; but since there is no agreement about the meaning of this term it is probably best to avoid it (see John Rogerson, *Genesis 1-11,* 55).

Genesis 1-11 is, as a literary work, more than the sum of its parts. In order to understand its nature and purpose it is first necessary to take a preliminary look at its contents. These may be summarized as follows (slightly different distribution of the topics is possible):

1:1–2:4a:	An account of the creation by God (Elohim) of the heavens and the earth and all the species of flora and fauna including humankind
2:4b-25:	An account of the creation by the Lord God (Yahweh Elohim) of the first man and woman and his placing them in a "garden in Eden" to till it and manage it
3:1-24:	Story of the eating of a forbidden fruit by the man and woman at the instigation of a cunning snake, and their consequent expulsion from the garden
4:1-16:	Story of Cain's murder of his brother Abel and his banishment by Yahweh
4:17-22:	List of descendants of Cain
4:23-24:	Lamech's song
4:25–5:32:	Lists of descendants of Seth
6:1-4:	Story of the union of the "sons of God" with human women and the appearance of the giants (Nephilim)
6:5–9:17:	Story of God's decision to destroy a corrupted humanity

30

by a flood, the sending of that flood, the rescue of Noah
and his family in an ark, and the institution of a new
beginning for humankind

9:18-29: The sons of Noah, his drunkenness, and his death

10:1-32: List of descendants of Noah's sons (the "Table of the
Nations")

11:1-9: Story of an arrogant attempt by mankind (literally, "the
whole earth") to build a city and a tower "with its top in
the heavens" and Yahweh's frustration of their project by
scattering them throughout the earth and "confusing
their language," so rendering mutual communication impossible for them (the story of the "Tower of Babel")

11:10-30: List of descendants of Shem

11:31-32: Migration of Terah, Abram, Lot, and Sarai from Ur of
the Chaldeans to Haran

It has been suggested that the final author or compiler of these
chapters has left an indication of the structure of the work in his use of
the Hebrew word *toledoth*, especially in the phrase "These are the *toledoth*
of. . . ." This, or comparable phrases, occurs in Gen. 2:4 ("of the heavens
and the earth"); 5:1 ("of Adam"); 6:9 ("of Noah"); 10:1 ("of the sons of
Noah"); 11:10 ("of Shem"); 11:27 ("of Terah"). Its use was not, however,
confined to chs. 1-11; the phrase occurs also several times in the later
chapters of Genesis with regard to Ishmael (25:12), Isaac (25:19), Esau
(36:1, 9), Jacob (37:2, where RSV reads "This is the *history* of the family
of Jacob"). It cannot, however, be regarded as a basic structural marker
either of chs. 1-11 or of the whole book of Genesis. One reason is that
the word *toledoth* is used, in these chapters as elsewhere, in more than
one distinct sense, and with more than one distinct function. Its most
frequent sense is that of "descendants" or "list of descendants"
(genealogy); here its function is to introduce a list of names (Adam, Cain,
Lamech, Seth, Noah, Shem). But elsewhere it appears to mean "history"
or "narrative." For example, "These are the *toledoth* of the heavens and
the earth when they were created" (the only occurrence of the phrase
where it is not associated with personal names) in 2:4 appears to be a
reference to *events* (i.e., to God's creative acts). Moreover, its function
here is not introductory but summarizing; it forms the *conclusion* of a
narrative. In 37:2 "These are the *toledoth* of Jacob" also refers to a
narrative rather than to a list of names; but in that case it *precedes* the

31

narrative of the chapters which follow, which recount the history of the family of Jacob-Joseph and his brothers.

Clearly the "*toledoth* series" cannot be regarded as a reliable indication of the structure of Gen. 1-11. It is not, in fact, a coherent system; the term *toledoth* has been used here in several quite different ways. But this does not mean that these chapters have no comprehensive structure.

One way of discerning the structure of Gen. 1-11 is to note the fluctuation in the relationship — if one may so call it — between the principal characters, God and his human creatures. This fluctuation can perhaps be most clearly seen in some of the words spoken by these characters and the comments of the narrator. For example,

Narrator (1:27): So God created humankind (Hebrew *adham*) in his own image.

Narrator (1:31): God saw everything that he had made, and behold, it was very good.

God to the man (2:16-17): You may freely eat of every tree in the garden; but of the tree of the knowledge of good and evil you must not eat, for in the day that you eat of it you will surely die.

Snake to the woman (3:4-5): You will not die; for God knows that when you eat of it your eyes will be opened, and you will be like God, knowing good and evil.

God to the man (3:17-19): Because you . . . have eaten of the tree which I commanded you that you should not eat of it, cursed is the ground because of you.

God to himself (3:22): Behold, the man has become like one of us, knowing good and evil; and now, lest he put forth his hand and take also from the tree of life, and eat, and live for ever. . . .

Narrator (3:23): Therefore the Lord God sent him forth from the garden of Eden to till the ground from which he had been taken.

Narrator (4:8): Cain rose up against his brother Abel, and killed him.

God to Cain (4:12): You will be a fugitive and a wanderer on the earth.

Narrator (4:15): But the Lord put a mark on Cain, so that no one who came upon him would kill him.

Narrator (4:26): At that time people began to call upon the name of the Lord.

Narrator (5:24): Enoch walked with God; then he was no more, for God took him.

Narrator (6:5): The Lord saw that human wickedness was great . . . and that every inclination of the thoughts of their hearts was only evil continually.

God to himself (6:7): I shall blot out from the earth the human beings that I have created . . . , for I regret that I made them.

Narrator (6:8): But Noah found favor in the eyes of the Lord.

Narrator (6:9): Noah walked with God.

God to himself (8:21): I will never again curse the ground . . . nor will I ever again destroy every living creature as I have done.

God to Noah (9:11-12): I establish my covenant with you . . . for all generations.

Narrator (9:20-21): Noah . . . became drunk, and he lay uncovered in his tent.

"The whole earth" (= all mankind) (11:4): Let us build ourselves a city, and a tower with its top in the heavens, and let us make a name for ourselves.

God to himself (11:6): Behold, . . . this is only the beginning of what they will do; nothing that they plan to do will be impossible for them.

Narrator (11:8-9): The Lord scattered them abroad . . . over the face of all the earth, and they left off building the city. Therefore it was called Babel, because the Lord confused the language of all the earth.

Looking back on the above data, one may say that the author presents the reader with a rather unexpected portrait of God. Despite the assurance at the beginning (1:31) that when God surveyed his creative actions he concluded that the result was wholly good, God appears quite soon to be somewhat nervous about what he has done and, in particular, concerned about his own supremacy over his creatures. He sets conditions to mankind's freedom (2:17) and threatens immediate death as a consequence of disobedience, a threat that the snake — quite correctly, as it turns out — flatly rejects, calling God a liar. When the act of disobedience has been committed, God betrays nervousness about the possibility that mankind may now go further and seize the immortality which properly belongs only to God (3:22). The same anxiety betrays itself in the final episode of these chapters (11:6), when God fears that mankind may succeed in wresting unlimited (i.e., divine) power for themselves. In both cases God takes steps to forestall these ambitions. Meanwhile the mysterious incident of the union of the "sons of God" with the daughters of men (6:1-2) also seems to have been regarded by God as containing a threat of immortality human or semi-divine (compare 3:22), which needed to be suppressed.

It is in keeping with this presentation of the divine character that God is credited with a change of mind, and one of crucial importance for mankind. He regrets that he created them and determines to destroy them (6:7) because they have become irredeemably wicked (6:5). Creating them, then, was a mistake; the God who had at first assessed his own creative work as perfect had been unable to foresee what it would become. Throughout most of this narrative God appears to be reacting at every turn to what mankind was doing rather than taking the initiative. Fortunately for mankind (and God?), Noah turned out to be an exception to the general depravity (6:8, 9), and a new beginning became possible.

An alternative way of viewing the purpose and structure of chs. 1-11, however, is that it presents a picture of "the growing power of sin in the world," together with a parallel picture of "a hidden growth of grace" (so Gerhard von Rad, "The Form-Critical Problem of the Hexateuch," 64, 65). This view has some plausibility as regards chs. 2-9: the initial act of disobedience is followed by the first murder, then by the boast of Lamech that he will wreak vengeance not merely seven but seventy-seven times (4:24), and finally by the total and irredeemable depravity of mankind in ch. 6. It might also be argued that although there is a corresponding increase in the severity of the punishments inflicted on the sinners, culminating in the virtually total destruction of mankind, the extent of the divine grace and forgiveness also expands, culminating in ch. 9 with the blessing given to Noah and his descendants and the covenant made by God not only with these but also with all living creatures (9:12), coupled with God's promise never again to destroy mankind or to disrupt the normal course of a beneficent nature (8:21-22).

But if such a pattern is in fact to be found here, it surely comes to an end in 9:17. The story of the Flood and the (partial) restoration of (what is left of) humanity to something resembling the close relationship with God portrayed in ch. 2 marks a satisfactory conclusion to the whole "universal history." The view of von Rad ("The Form-Critical Problem of the Hexateuch," 66, n. 107) that it is the story of the Tower of Babel (11:1-9) which marks "the climax of the whole section" is not well founded. Rather than a climax, the scattering of humanity and the confusion of their speech, though hardly propitious for mankind's future, came rather as an anticlimax after the story of their almost total destruction in the Flood. Indeed, one might suppose that the story of the Tower of Babel is a kind of author's afterthought.

However, it is probably best to regard it as an appendix to chs. 1-9, included as a final parable of human sin and God's response. It is significant that the Tower of Babel account contains no proper names and mentions no individuals at all; after the plethora of proper names (especially in ch. 10) this story seems to move in a different world. The builders of the city and tower are curiously called "the whole earth" (v. 1) and "they" (v. 2). The story is a powerful parable about the fate that awaits human rebelliousness, ambition, and arrogance — a timeless narrative akin to the fairy story. But in its present position it also balances — and corrects — ch. 1 with its insistence that what God created was "very good."

Genesis 1-11, then, is not merely concerned with speculating about the remote past — about "how it might have been" when the world began. These chapters have clearly been composed with an eye to what was to follow: the somewhat more recent past and the history of God's chosen people. They do not, it is true, mention the people of Israel, which had not yet come into existence; they are about mankind in general — a universal history — but they end with an unmistakable presage of what is to come. With 11:10 there is a resumption of the genealogical lists, with a list of the descendants of Shem. Toward the end of that chapter we encounter Terah, the father of Abram. Finally in v. 31 we are told that Terah, together with his son Abram, his grandson Lot (the son of Haran), and Abram's wife Sarai migrated from his home in Ur of the Chaldeans to go into the land of Canaan, but that they went only part of the way and settled in Haran. With this information we have been introduced to the principal characters of the chapters which immediately follow, in particular, to the ancestors of Israel — to "Abraham our father" and to Sarah, who was to become the mother of the promised heir Isaac and the ancestress of the nation. With this, the prologue to the Pentateuch is at an end.

What is the point of this prologue? Why did the author of the Pentateuch begin his history of Israel's ancestors with these chapters?

In attempting to answer these questions, it may first be pointed out that histories of particular nations or peoples which began with an account of the origins of the world and then, by genealogical or other means, linked this to "historical" times were not entirely unusual in ancient literature. Israel was by no means unique in this respect. This is especially true of some of the early Greek historians of the sixth and fifth centuries B.C. (see John Van Seters, *In Search of History,* 8ff.). But the very early Sumerian King List (ca. 1800-1600; *ANET,* 265-66), which begins with the words "When kingship was lowered from heaven," immediately proceeds with a list of clearly legendary kings there stated to have reigned "before the Flood" for an incredible number of years (e.g., Alalgar, 36,000 years; cf., though in less extravagant style, the lifespans in Gen. 5 and 11:10-25) before descending to more "historical" kings with reigns of "normal" lengths. The so-called Creation Epic *(Enuma Elish)* from Babylonia *(ANET,* 60-72) represents the creator-god Marduk as having subsequently ordered and carried out the building of the undoubtedly historical city of Babylon so that he might be worshipped there. Similar "histories" that proceed from the mythical origins of the world to accounts of actual historical persons and events can also be cited from other parts of the world — for example, the Japanese *Kojiki,* "Chronicle of Ancient Times."

Evidently an interest in the way in which the world and humankind came into existence and in the history of the earliest times was characteristic of the ancient civilized world. At any rate, various "origin stories" or "creation myths" about the activities of a variety of creator-gods are still extant in what remains of the literatures of ancient Egypt and ancient Mesopotamia. But the combination of such accounts with narratives about more recent times testifies to an additional motivation. The aim of such works was to give their readers — or to strengthen — a sense of national or ethnic *identity,* particularly at a time when there was for some reason a degree of uncertainty or hesitation about this. Such works are basically *national* or ethnic histories rather than universal ones: the center of interest is a particular ethnic group. In order to foster a sense of identity it was necessary to create an understanding of the place of that nation or people *in the world* — that is, among the other nations in the world whose existence was acknowledged and with which some kind of relations were necessary, but which were felt to be alien. It was therefore important to know how a humanity that was believed to have had a single origin had become divided into separate nations and had developed different customs and languages. In the case of Gen. 1-11, this theme — already hinted at in the various genealogies — is explicitly dealt with in ch. 10, evidently intended as a comprehensive list of the peoples of the world and the locations to which they had migrated, and in 11:1-9, which accounts for their failure to remain united and gives the reason for their dispersal and their subsequent mutual alienation through inability to communicate with one another.

The placing of Gen. 1-11 as a prologue to the main body of the work also afforded the opportunity to express certain distinctively Israelite articles of faith which it would have been more difficult to introduce into the later narratives, particularly with regard to the doctrine of God. Specifically, although the creation narratives of chs. 1 and 2 have unmistakable affinities with those of other Near Eastern peoples (see below), the monotheistic character of all these chapters is quite striking and even polemical, despite the isolated "Let *us* make mankind in *our* image" of 1:26 and "like one of us" in 3:22. Ch. 1 contains further examples of a polemical or anti-polytheistic stance. For example, whereas in the Babylonian *Enuma Elish* the stars are divine beings (Tablet V, lines 1ff.; *ANET,* 67), in Gen. 1:14-18 the heavenly bodies are merely created objects set in the sky with specific functions to perform. Again, the "great sea monsters" (Hebrew *tanninim,* 1:21), elsewhere in the Old Testament (Ps. 74:13-14; Isa. 51:9) presented as adversaries that God had to fight and kill (a tradition found also in the non-Israelite literature, e.g., *Enuma Elish,* Tablet IV, lines 101ff.), simply appear as his creatures. Here we have a "demythologization" of polytheistic beliefs held both in Israel and elsewhere. There are other polemical traits in these chapters — for example, in the story of the Flood — which point to a time of composition when Israel's theology, already monotheistic, had been again subject to insidious polytheistic notions, especially those of Babylonian origin.

Some scholars have gone further and seen the narratives of Gen. 1-11 as a whole to be reflecting the experiences of the Babylonian Exile or the early postexilic period. Thus the themes of punishment for sin, especially banishment from God's presence and/or dispersal or destruction (3:23-24; 4:12, 16; 6-8; 11:4, 9), have been taken as symbolic of Israel's richly deserved banishment from the land of Canaan. The signs of grace and forgiveness, especially God's acceptance of Noah's sacrifice and the covenant which God made with him (8:20–9:17), would, it has been supposed, suggest to the exilic/postexilic reader that God has even now not cast off his people but is a God of infinite patience and forgiveness who may yet again rescue them from their folly and their guilt. Such an allegorical interpretation of these chapters, however, perhaps reads more into them than their author intended.

These stories also betray an interest in etiology — in seeking the origin of various phenomena of universal human experience which appear to defy explanation. This kind of questioning ("Why?") is a further indication of the breadth of approach of this "universal history." The questions raised (by implication) here are almost all questions concerning the basic aspects of human existence, and have been taken to reflect a kind of universal "wisdom" or seeking after truth not confined to any one people.

(The genealogical lists in these chapters, of course, also imply that in view of their common descent all human beings are, in one sense, "brothers.")

The etiologies offered in these chapters are of many kinds. The question about the reason for human mortality, a common theme in both Near Eastern and classical thought which sometimes took the form of narratives in which human beings attempted to wrest immortality from the gods but failed, is alluded to in 3:22 — which appears to imply that mortality is inherent in mankind's status as creature — and in the mysterious incident of 6:1-3. It would therefore seem that mortality was not held to be a punishment for human disobedience, although it is probably significant that the first human death recorded — inflicted by a fellow human being — occurred immediately after the expulsion from the garden.

The nature of the relationship between man and woman is discussed in 2:18, which explains why both sexes are necessary to a complete humanity, and in 2:23-24, which explains the attraction between the sexes and the forming of permanent relationships between them as due to God's providence. (Note the word "Therefore" in v. 24 — an explicit introduction to an etiology, answering the here unspoken question, "Why?"). But in ch. 3 the less ideal realities of the relationship as we know it are attributed to the disobedience to God's command, in which both the man and the woman (as well as the snake) are equally involved. V. 16, which is the first reference to childbearing, provides an explanation of women's labor pains, and also of men's dominance over women.

There is also an etiology of work here. Work in itself is not regarded as a punishment. Instead, it is a natural and essential (male) activity (2:15), but — it is implied — a pleasant one. Life in the garden is pleasant (2:9). The cursing of the ground and the consequent harshness of agricultural labor (3:17-19) are the result of the act of disobedience; the final line of v. 19 ("You are dust, and to dust you shall return"), possibly a common saying, does not imply that human mortality is the result of disobedience (see the discussion in Gerhard von Rad, *Genesis*).

Another matter which evidently needed explanation was the phenomenon of human clothing. The feelings of shame at appearing naked before others (cf. 9:20-27) and the assumption of the need for clothes are explained as a consequence of the man and the woman having eaten of the forbidden fruit of the tree of knowledge (3:7-12, 21); it is specifically stated that previously they had not been ashamed of their nakedness (2:25). Other etiologies in these chapters include the cause of the general human dislike of snakes and also of snakes' ability to move without legs (3:14-15) and the reason for the existence of the rainbow (9:12-17).

An etiology which is wholly peculiar to Israel is that of the origin of the sabbath, unmistakably implied in 2:1-3 in the statement that God blessed and declared holy the seventh day, on which he rested from his creative work. This is an example of a tendency observable elsewhere in the Pentateuch (e.g., in many of the laws, and in particular in the description of the tabernacle in the wilderness [Exod. 25ff.], which was in many respects an anticipation of Solomon's temple) to ascribe the earliest conceivable time to the establishment of a religious institution.

To assign a date or historical setting to these chapters is not possible with any degree of certainty. They are, in a sense, timeless. Source criticism seems hardly relevant here; in some form these stories could have arisen at almost any time in the history of Israel. Certain features in the text as it now stands, however, point to a fairly late date. This applies not only to the sections which the documentary critics label as P, but also to the sections attributed to the preexilic sources J and E. While some theories (e.g., that the theme of banishment from God's presence reflects the exilic period) are speculative and unprovable, references like that to Ur of the Chaldeans in Gen. 11:28, 31 seem to rule out an early date in view of the late appearance of the Chaldeans on the international stage. There are other pointers, not conclusive but nevertheless suggestive, of a late recension. For example, it is somewhat strange that the garden of Eden is nowhere mentioned in preexilic Old Testament texts but appears only in the exilic Isaiah ("Deutero-Isaiah"), Ezekiel (where ch. 28 has a variant version of the Eden story), Joel, and Habakkuk. Further, the dependence on Mesopotamian traditions evident in several chapters raises the question how these could have been known to an Israelite writer before the period of Babylonian influence on Israel — from the late seventh century at the earliest. It is, however, of course possible that much of the material may have existed in some form some time before its inclusion in these chapters. If the Pentateuch is to be regarded as a single work, these considerations are significant for the dating of the work as a whole. John Van Seters's remark about the patriarchal stories that "there is nothing in this presentation . . . which is inappropriate to . . . the period of the late Judean monarchy or exilic periods, but there is much that speaks against the choice of any earlier period" should be borne in mind (*Abraham in History and Tradition*, 38).

It is generally agreed that the stories in Gen. 1-11 are not a pure invention of the author. However much he may have adapted them to his own purposes, he clearly made use of traditional themes currently circulating in his own time. Where had these originated? First, it is important to note that there is no extant ancient Near Eastern text that in any way covers the same ground as Gen. 1-11 — that is, that covers all the main episodes — and no evidence that any other people compiled a comparable narrative before the Graeco-Roman period, when there was an interest in such matters and works of this kind may well have become quite common. Berossus (third century) included such material in a history of Babylon, Manetho (second century) similarly in a history of Egypt, and Philo of Byblos (first-second century A.D.) in his *Phoenician History.* These works, all written in Greek and unfortunately preserved only in comparatively brief quotations in other works, attempted to link traditional stories about the doings of the gods with later historical events. Some earlier Greek works had already made efforts in this direction. Hesiod's *Works and Days* (probably eighth century B.C.) was a precursor, and the later Greek historians Hecataeus and Hellanicus, whose works also are preserved only in fragmentary form, carried the enterprise further (see Van Seters, *In Search of History,* 8-18). But there is no evidence of comparable works from Egypt or Mesopotamia before the Hellenistic period. There was, however, an abundance of unconnected stories from those quarters about such matters as the creation of the world, the creation of mankind, the Flood, and other "primeval" events.

Genesis 1:1–2:4a

This creation story is only one of many current in the ancient Near East. For example, there are several Egyptian stories extant in which the creation of the world is attributed to different gods, and the creator-god is not necessarily the principal god — a multiplicity which is due to different local traditions. Also in Israel itself, where there is only one creator, who has supreme power and no rivals, there are several different versions. In addition to Gen. 1 and 2, there is another version of which traces appear in various contexts, in which the creation appears to have followed a conflict wherein Yahweh defeated or killed a sea monster or monsters (especially Ps. 74:13-17; Isa. 51:9), and yet other versions in Prov. 8:22-31, in parts of the book of Job, and elsewhere.

The creation story in Gen. 1:1–2:4a has long been thought to have particular affinities with *Enuma Elish* (*ANET,* 60-72); but a glance at the Mesopotamian myth shows that the relationship is at most a very remote one. Apart from the fact that the Genesis story is monotheistic, a crucial difference between the two accounts is that *Enuma Elish* belongs to the category of the conflict tradition, which is entirely absent from the Genesis account. In *Enuma Elish* Marduk is able to create the world only by summoning his allies and killing the sea monster Tiamat and her allies; heaven and earth are created by the splitting of Tiamat's body into two. The commonly repeated notion that the Hebrew word translated "the deep" (*tehom,* Gen. 1:2) is a pale reminiscence of Tiamat cannot be sustained. There is no trace of a conflict here; God is alone, and he is supreme. There is no explicit statement in the Genesis narrative about God's purpose in creating the world. However, this purpose is clearly implied in the great emphasis that is placed on the position of mankind in God's plan: the creation of mankind, the last of God's creative acts, is evidently the climax of the whole account, and receives the greatest attention. That which was created on previous days — light, day and night, dry land, heavenly bodies, plants and animals — are all by implication provided for mankind's use and convenience. Mankind is given the plants for food and power over the animal creation. Above all, mankind is created in God's *image* and *likeness.* Whatever may be the precise meaning of these terms (this question has been endlessly debated), they set mankind apart from all the other creatures and put them in a unique relationship with God himself. In none of the other creation stories with which this story can be compared is such a high status attributed to mankind.

In its cosmology — that is, its understanding of the different parts of the universe and their relationship to one another — Gen. 1 conforms to the view generally accepted in the ancient Near East. (In other passages in the Old Testament this cosmology is described more fully.) The pre-existent watery waste (1:1-2) was divided into two by the creation of a solid dome or vault (the sky, v. 8) so that there was water both above and below it. The water below was then confined to a limited area, the sea, revealing the dry land, which God called "the earth." (According to the story of the Flood, 7:11, the sky had "windows" which when opened allowed the rain to fall.) The heavenly bodies, sun, moon, and stars, moved across the vault of the sky.

A characteristic feature of Gen. 1 in which it differs from other creation stories, both Israelite and non-Israelite, is its neatness and the precision of its presentation of the acts of creation. Using the same phraseology repeatedly, it lists these with the dryness of a catalogue. It has, for example, nothing of the drama or the imaginative skill of ch. 2. It gives the impression of an account which has been carefully honed and reduced systematically to a minimum. Yet, as Claus Westermann and others have pointed out, there remain certain variations in detail. Thus the creative acts are introduced in two different ways. In some cases God creates simply by speaking: "And God said. . . ." In others we are told that God performed certain actions: he made, separated, named, blessed, placed. A second "untidy" feature is that although the entire work of creation was carried out in six days (to conform with the concept of a week of action followed by a sabbath rest on the seventh day), there are in fact eight creative acts: on the third day and again on the sixth two acts of creation are performed. These features suggest that the account in its present form is based on earlier accounts in which the work of creation was originally performed in different ways, although there is now no way in which these earlier accounts can be reconstructed.

Genesis 2:4b–3:24

It is evident that this narrative, which could stand by itself as a complete and independent story, has taken up themes and motifs quite different from those employed in ch. 1. It was once generally believed to be older and more "primitive" in its theology than ch. 1 (J as contrasted with P). But more recently it has been doubted whether its "naiveté" is in fact more than apparent. Joseph Blenkinsopp, for example, sees the narrative as "generated by reflection on the creation account in Genesis 1" and as standing in a wisdom tradition which indulged in "what Plato called 'philosophizing by means of myth'" (*The Pentateuch*, 63, 65). Undoubtedly some of the motifs employed are themselves considerably older than the rather late period of composition postulated above; but it is true that the telling of tales for edifying or didactic purposes is a characteristic of a late state of civilization rather than an early one. There is evidence, too, that some of the vocabulary used in these chapters is distinctively late rather than early.

This is primarily a story about two people, a man and a woman, and what happened to them. Although these people are, in the context, necessarily pictured as the first man and woman, they are clearly symbols as well as ancestors of the human race itself. Behind his statements that "this is what happened," the author is saying "this is how human beings behave, and these are the consequences that follow": the eating of the fruit is not a single event in the remote past, but something that is repeated again and again in human history. There is thus here a series of lessons, applicable to human beings in general, but also in particular to the history of Israel. God's intention for the human beings that he has created is wholly good, but they can be led away by subtle temptation. Also, disobedience to God, which is self-assertion, may bring greater self-knowledge, but it leads to disaster. The intimate relationship with God is broken, and life then becomes harsh and unpleasant. However, even then God does not entirely abandon his creatures but makes special provisions for their future life. An Israel which had suffered devastation and exile from their land as a result of their disobedience to God could hardly fail to get the message.

It is hardly correct to call ch. 2 a "second creation story" as is frequently done, if by that is meant that this is an account of the creation of the world alternative to that of ch. 1. Rather, ch. 2 is concerned with the creation of human beings, and the reference to the creation of the world (which occupies only vv. 4b-6) simply provides the setting for that. This account clearly originally belonged to a different tradition from ch. 1 with its Babylonian perspective. The perspective here is that of Palestine, where rain was crucially important for the fertilization of plant life. But the author of chs. 2 and 3 has assembled a whole battery of different traditions to adorn his narrative.

In 2:7 the author chose to describe the creation of humankind in terms of their formation from the soil (perhaps rather, clay). It is not possible to identify the particular tradition that he used: Westermann pointed out that this is a common notion among primitive peoples. From the civilized ancient Near East we know of the Egyptian god Khnum, who fashions living creatures on a potter's wheel (see *ANET,* 368, 431, 441), and from Mesopotamia there is a reference to the creation of the wild man Enkidu from clay (*Gilgamesh,* Tablet I, ii, 30ff.; *ANET,* 74).

The references to the tree of the knowledge of good and evil (Gen. 2:9, 17 and presumably also 3:3, 11, 12) and to the tree of life (2:9; 3:22) constitute a puzzle, in that the latter does not appear in the main story but only in the two verses mentioned. The problem is usually, and probably rightly, solved by supposing that the author knowingly combined two separate traditions and was not much concerned with consistency of detail. This is not the only inconsistency in these chapters, and it would not be appropriate to speak either of a combination of literary sources or of subsequent additions made to a completed text.

Both trees have connections with wisdom themes. Knowledge is a synonym for wisdom in the book of Proverbs, and in Prov. 3:18 it is stated that wisdom is a "a tree of life to those who lay hold of her." This might lead one to suppose that the two trees were the same, were it not for the statement in Gen. 2:9 and 3:22 that they were distinct.

The themes of knowledge and of immortality have in common the fact that the attempt to attain either is an attempt to obtain what God has not given to mankind and so to encroach on the divine prerogative. In the Old Testament wisdom is an ambiguous quality, which may be used either for good purposes or for evil ones. In 3:1 for example, the wisdom possessed by the snake (said to be *arum*, "shrewd") is not presented as admirable. Indeed, the whole of this story could be interpreted as a warning that the acquisition of knowledge leads to disaster — a kind of counter-blast to the optimistic teaching of the book of Proverbs, for which the acquisition of wisdom is essential to human happiness.

The human desire for immortality (presupposed by God in Gen. 3:22) is a well-known theme in Mesopotamian literature. These texts lay stress on its inevitable frustration, and sometimes explicitly or implicitly counsel contentment with one's lot in the present life (see especially the *Epic of Gilgamesh,* Tablet XI, iii; *ANET,* 90). In this story the hero Gilgamesh actually secures the plant which confers eternal life, but it is then stolen from him by a snake, so incidentally accounting for the belief that snakes do possess immortality (the parallels with Gen. 2-3 are easy to see). Another story of failure to attain immortality, this time through dissension among the gods, is that of Adapa, who is offered the bread and water of life by the sky-god Anu but refuses it because he has been warned by the god of knowledge and wisdom not to accept it. In the Genesis story the supreme god has no rivals, but himself takes decisive measures to exclude mankind from the possibility of securing immortality.

The snake in this story is an enigmatic figure. It never appears again in the Old Testament. Westermann, probably rightly, sees this motif of a talking snake as a "fairy tale trait," probably very ancient, of which the author made use (*Genesis 1-11,* 238). Since it is clearly stated in 3:1 that the snake was simply one of the creatures that God had made, there is no justification for seeing it either as a supernatural enemy of God — the Devil or Satan — or as some kind of "inner voice" within the woman questioning God's intentions and urging her to do evil. It is best to see it as the text itself appears to do, as a creature, endowed by God with unusual intelligence and using this to oppose his wish. But it is pointless to expect precise logic here. If the snake was introduced into the story to account for the action of the woman, there is still nothing to account for the behavior of the snake, which was equally God's creature. (The dialogue between the snake and the woman, however — the first example of such a conversation in the Bible — is brilliantly achieved.)

However, snakes played a significant part in the mythologies and religious practices of the ancient Near East, and it was probably for this reason that the snake motif was introduced into this story. Snakes were objects both of fear and of worship, and Israel seems to have been no exception in this respect. The story in Num. 21:6-9, in which Moses at God's command set up a bronze snake in the wilderness to act as an antidote against the bites of poisonous snakes, illustrates both aspects of this attitude. The action of King Hezekiah in smashing the bronze snake called Nehushtan, specifically stated to be the one made by Moses, to which sacrifices had traditionally been offered in the Jerusalem temple (2 Kgs. 18:4) indicates the hold that this object had had among the Judeans. The snake in Gen. 3 may be a reflection of the abhorrence in which this form of idolatry was held in later times.

Genesis 6:1–9:29

Stories of a great flood sent in primeval times by gods to destroy mankind followed by some form of new creation are so common to so many peoples in different parts of the world, between whom no kind of historical contact seems possible, that the notion seems almost to be a universal feature of the human imagination. The Flood story of Genesis is a clear example of a type which was characteristic of the Mesopotamian world. The two extant literary accounts which it most closely resembles are *Atra-ḫasīs* (see the translation by Wilfred G. Lambert and Allan R. Millard) and Tablet XI of the *Epic of Gilgamesh* (*ANET*, 93-95). *Gilgamesh* is extant in more than one version. The Babylonian text, translated in *ANET* and first announced in 1872 by George Smith, caused a sensation because of its astonishing resemblance in detail to the Genesis story. According to Lambert and Millard (p. 11), it was largely derived from the account in *Atra-ḫasīs*. Tablet XI of Gilgamesh is not connected with a creation story and appears to have been borrowed from an earlier text. *Atra-ḫasīs*, though in its fragmentary state it lacks some of the details (especially the sending out of birds to discover whether the water has receded), is closer to Genesis in that it contains an account of the creation of mankind from clay before proceeding to the story of the Flood.

It has long been pointed out that Gen. 6-9 contains a number of details such as the chronology of the Flood and the numbers of animals taken into the ark which are in contradiction. Attempts to reconcile these, however ingenious, can hardly be convincing. It is clear that more than one version have been combined. The question is, at what time and by whom the combination was carried out. The text cannot be separated into two complete versions. If the story as we have it is rigidly divided into two sources, one of these would obviously have been only partially preserved; there is, for example, only one account of the embarkation in the ark, without which there can be no story. Rather than two written sources, it is then the author himself — who probably knew a number of versions from which he could choose — who has spliced two of them together without concerning himself with all the details. We have observed the use of the same method in his treatment of chs. 2-3.

As has already been noted, in Genesis the Flood story is the climax of a sequence which begins with creation and ends, after total disaster for mankind, on a positive note with the renewal of mankind through Noah and his sons. This renewal of mankind is not to be found either in the *Epic of Gilgamesh* or *Atra-ḥasīs*. In *Gilgamesh* the Flood is only an episode. The story is told by Utnapishtim, who alone is saved; but far from becoming the ancestor of new humanity, Utnapishtim is banished to a place "far away, at the mouth of the rivers," where he lives alone, and to which Gilgamesh travels in a vain attempt to obtain for himself that immortality. *Atra-ḥasīs,* like Gen. 6-9, is also part of a sequence of events, but one which is quite different from that of Genesis. It begins with a revolt of the gods, who are overburdened with work, and with the creation of mankind so that they may be given the work to do in place of the gods. The occasion of the Flood is the tremendous noise made by mankind, who have become numerous and disturb the sleep of the gods, who then attempt unsuccessfully to reduce the human population by sending plague, famine, and drought on the earth before determining to destroy mankind altogether by a Flood. The man Atra-ḥasīs alone survives; the end of the account is missing. These differences from the Genesis story, together with the fact that in these nonbiblical versions there is constant quarrelling among the gods, who attempt to frustrate one another's activities, bring out both the simplicity and the theological distinctiveness of the account in Genesis.

The genealogical lists in these chapters comprise a very substantial part of the whole. They are more than simply links in a chain spanning the period from Adam to Abraham. Like so much of the material, they belong to a Near Eastern tradition which included theogonies — lists showing the genealogical relationships between the gods — but also lists of kings, including kings said to have reigned "before the Flood" or who "lived in tents" (for the king lists, see *ANET,* 265-66, Sumerian; 564-66, Assyrian; 271-74, Babylonian). However, the early parts of these lists, covering the primeval period, are not genealogical but are simply names of successive kings. The lists go down to historical times. Recent study of the subject has begun to take into account also oral genealogies transmitted within modern tribal societies; but much work remains to be done (see Robert R. Wilson, "The Old Testament Genealogies in Recent Research").

The lists in Gen. 1-11 are not entirely consistent. There are, for example, two different genealogies of Adam, one through Cain (4:17ff.) and one through Seth (5:3ff.). Both lists, however, include some of the same or similar names. Both the non-biblical and modern oral genealogies show similar inconsistencies. It is clear that such genealogies are fluid; in the course of time they have come to serve different purposes, often political or concerned with relationships between tribes, and have been altered accordingly. In the case of Gen. 1-11, the genealogy of Cain seems to be related to the theme of a general human deterioration which was the cause of the Flood. It ends with the sinister figure of Lamech (4:23-24). On the contrary, the genealogy of Seth, which includes Enoch (who "walked with God," 5:24), ends with the savior of the human race, Noah, and his family. The author was of course aware of the inconsistencies, but used the lists for different purposes.

For Further Reading

Blenkinsopp, Joseph. *The Pentateuch: An Introduction to the First Five Books of the Bible.* New York: Doubleday and London: SCM, 1992, ch 3.

Brandon, S. G. F. *Creation Legends of the Ancient Near East.* London: Hodder & Stoughton, 1963.

Frankfort, Henri, *et al. The Intellectual Adventure of Ancient Man.* Chicago: University of Chicago Press, 1946. Repr. 1977.

Heidel, Alexander. *The Babylonian Genesis: The Story of the Creation.* 2nd ed. Chicago: University of Chicago Press, 1963.

Johnson, Marshall D. *The Purpose of the Biblical Genealogies.* SNTS Monograph 8. Cambridge: Cambridge University Press, 1969. 2nd ed., 1988.

Lambert, Wilfred G., and Millard, Allan R. *Atra-ḫasīs: The Babylonian Story of the Flood.* Oxford: Clarendon, 1969.

von Rad, Gerhard. "The Form-Critical Problem of the Hexateuch," in *The Problem of the Hexateuch and Other Essays.* Edinburgh: Oliver & Boyd, 1966, 1-78. Repr. Philadelphia: Fortress and London: SCM, 1984. (First published in German, 1938.)

———. *Genesis.* 3rd ed. OTL. Philadelphia: Westminster and London: SCM, 1972. (9th German ed., 1972.)

Rendtorff, Rolf. *The Old Testament: An Introduction.* London: SCM, 1985, and Philadelphia: Fortress, 1986. (First published in German, 1983.)

Rogerson, John. *Genesis 1-11.* OTG. Sheffield: JSOT Press, 1991.

Skinner, John. *A Critical and Exegetical Commentary on Genesis.* 2nd ed. ICC. Edinburgh: T. & T. Clark, 1930.

Van Seters, John. *Abraham in History and Tradition.* New Haven: Yale University Press, 1975.

Wenham, Gordon J. *Genesis 1-15.* WBC 1. Waco: Word, 1987.

Westermann, Claus. *Creation.* Philadelphia: Fortress and London: SPCK, 1974. (First published in German, 1971.)

———. *Genesis: A Practical Commentary.* Grand Rapids: Wm. B. Eerdmans, 1987. (First published in Dutch, 1986.)

———. *Genesis 1-11.* Minneapolis: Augsburg and London: SPCK, 1984. (Translated from the 2nd German ed. in the *Biblischer Kommentar* series, 1976.)

———. *The Genesis Accounts of Creation.* Philadelphia: Fortress, 1964. (Translated from the 2nd German ed., 1961.)

Wilson, Robert R. "The Old Testament Genealogies in Recent Research," *JBL* 94 (1975): 169-189.

CHAPTER 4

The History of the Patriarchs (Genesis 12-50)

THE TIME SPAN of these chapters is comparatively short. They comprise the history of four generations of a single family: Abraham, his son Isaac, his grandson Jacob, and his twelve great-grandsons. These were of vital interest to the later Israelites because they believed them to be their own ancestors; they are often referred to simply as "the fathers." Abraham was the father of the nation, and his great-grandsons the founders of the twelve tribes, of which the nation was believed to consist. This patriarchal history is, however, only the first part of the story of the origins of the nation: it looks forward to the events recounted in the later books. Thus while the lives of Abraham, Isaac, and Jacob were passed mainly in Canaan, the story of Joseph with which the book of Genesis comes to an end (chs. 37-50) takes the whole family to live in Egypt. This sets the stage for the stories of the oppression of their descendants by the Egyptians and of the Exodus which are the subjects of the first chapters of the book of Exodus.

Where did the author obtain the material for his history? It is an astonishing fact that the preexilic parts of the Old Testament make no mention at all of the incidents connected with Abraham, Isaac, or Jacob with the sole exception of Hos. 12:3-4, 12, where the prophet shows familiarity with certain episodes in the life of Jacob. Although the names Isaac and Jacob were sometimes used in poetical texts (not prose ones) as designations of northern Israel, even bare references to them as individuals in texts that are certainly preexilic are extremely infrequent. It is only from the time of the Exile in the sixth century that we have texts (Isa. 51:2; Ezek. 33:24) that refer to Abraham as an individual, in connection with problems faced by the exiles or by those left in the land after the Babylonian conquest. This suggests that the stories about the patriarchs which the author of Genesis used in his history may for the most part be no older than that period. There is no evidence that they were current over a long period before then, and the fact that they are mentioned neither in the historical books nor by the preexilic prophets suggests the contrary.

At this point it is appropriate to consider the nature of historiography as it was understood in the ancient world. The ideal (never in fact attained) of recording, as far as this is possible, the "brute facts" or "what actually happened" in the past is a very modern one. Not only did an ancient historian set out with a preconceived aim — political, religious, moral, educative — in mind, which went beyond the recording of bare facts; the historian also considered it to be part of his function to arrange, embellish, and embroider the material to make it more attractive and exciting to the reader or in some way more palatable or moral, or to use it to make a religious point. This would necessitate at least a degree of invention, which in modern terms would be called fiction.

As is generally recognized, a large part of the narrative books of the Old Testament are literary fiction. This is true of the prologue and epilogue of the book of Job, the books of Ruth, Jonah, Esther, Daniel 1-6, and large parts of the books of Chronicles and probably of other narratives as well. Some of these stories are expansions of earlier narratives; this is the case, for example, with the additional material in Chronicles that expands the story of David. In other cases a whole story appears to be pure fiction. The book of Jonah takes a name about which nothing at all is known apart from a single verse in 2 Kgs. 14:25, and uses this name as a peg on which to hang an entire narrative with a religious message — an early example of what came later to be known as *midrash*. In the cases of Ruth, Esther, and Daniel there was, as far as we know, no such known name on which to hang these completely fictitious tales (though the name Daniel appears in Ezra 8:2 in a list of returned exiles). The parables of Jesus are also of course fiction. The story of Job is of particular relevance to our present inquiry because Job, who is universally recognized to be a wholly fictitious character, is portrayed as a patriarch similar to the Abraham of Genesis.

The fact that Abraham, Isaac, and Jacob have become such outstanding figures in both Judaism and Christianity may be due more to the skill of the narrator than to any ancient long-standing traditions that preceded him. That the figures of these patriarchs were originally unrelated to one another and have been used to create a fictitious "family history" is widely admitted. There is also a possibility that some of the stories attributed to one or other of these figures may have originally been told about some other legendary figures altogether. Such schematization smacks of the historical novelist rather than of a faithful transmitter of ancient traditions. If "patriarchal" stories like that of the prose narrative of the book of Job were circulating *in his time,* the author would have had material at hand which he could combine and expand, using them to create an account of Israel's ancestors with an appropriate religious message — a method analogous to that employed by the early Greek historians.

The view stated above, however, is not one that has commanded general assent. A series of scholars has continued to follow Hermann Gunkel's theory of *Sagen* or small units of an early period gradually combined to form the written sources J, (E), and P. This is true of Albrecht Alt ("The God of the Fathers," 1929, English translation 1967), Gerhard von Rad, and also of Claus Westermann.

Rolf Rendtorff and John Van Seters, in studies both published in 1975, rejected the "classical" source theory, but continued to support the notion of a series of stages leading to the final text of the patriarchal stories. In his work on the composition of the Pentateuch, Rendtorff did not clearly indicate at what period he believed the stories to have originated, though in a later (1982) article on the composition of one story (that of Jacob at Bethel, Gen. 28:10-22), he supported an earlier view that the core of this story is a (presumably rather early) "cult etiology" relating to the foundation of the sanctuary at Bethel, which subsequently underwent a series of changes and additions. Rendtorff's pupil, Erhard Blum, in a work wholly concerned with the patriarchal history (1984), added further precision: he saw no evidence to suggest that any of the stories predates the early monarchy, but he also believed that they had a fairly long and complex history. They were first combined in two recensions, a "history of Abraham" composed in Judah, and a "history of Jacob" from the northern kingdom. These were then combined in Judah in a "patriarchal history" which underwent two recensions, the first compiled before the Exile and the second in the late sixth century, before being incorporated into a "Deuteronomistic Pentateuch."

The view of Van Seters is not dissimilar to this. He postulated an exilic "J," but this had been preceded by an earlier written work. Van Seters also saw no evidence that the stories had been preserved from a "patriarchal age." He held that it is extremely difficult to distinguish between oral and written sources, but also pointed out that oral sources are not necessarily either early or preliterate. The crucial questions seem to be whether it is possible for traditions to be preserved orally for several hundred years, and whether the text as it stands can or cannot be accounted for as the work of a single author who incorporated his own theological comments and interpretations into material which was in some sense traditional.

It cannot be said that in combining these stories the author succeeded in producing an entirely coherent account of the lives of the patriarchs. A number of stories have been placed in inconsequent positions. This is particularly true of the Abraham stories (chs. 12-25), though the most incongruous of the dislocations occurs with the story of Judah and Tamar (ch. 38), which interrupts the otherwise well-constructed account of the life of Joseph (chs. 37-50). Nevertheless, in general an attempt has been made to present the stories in "chronological" sequence. The patriarchal history has been arranged in three main, more or less clearly defined, parts: the stories of Abraham (12:1–25:11), Jacob (25:21–35:29), and Joseph (chs. 37-50). The story of Jacob is itself clearly divided into three parts, corresponding to three stages in his life: the account of his relations with his immediate family, especially with his brother Esau (chs. 25-27, 32-35), is bisected by the story of Jacob's journeys and his relations with his uncle Laban (chs. 28-31).

It can hardly be said that there is an independent "story" of Isaac. The events of his life are narrated partly in the story of Abraham and partly in that of Jacob. As would be expected in a "family" history, there is also some overlap between all these "histories." Thus the death of Abraham (25:8) takes place only after the account of Isaac's marriage; Isaac's death (35:29) comes at the end of the story of Jacob; and Jacob's death (49:33) almost at the end of the story of Joseph. The death of Joseph is recorded in the final verse of the book (50:26).

The patriarchal history is interspersed with genealogies: of Nahor (22:20-24), of Abraham by his second wife (25:1-6), of Ishmael (25:12-16), of Jacob (35:22-26), of Esau (36:1-43, including also a list of kings of Edom), and again of Jacob (46:8-27). The main purpose of these genealogies is to claim Abraham and his family as ancestors of other peoples: Aramaeans, Moabites, Ammonites, Arabians, Ishmaelites, Hittites. The final list, however, prepares for the events of the book of Exodus by naming the descendants of Jacob who left Canaan to reside in Egypt.

The main theme of the patriarchal history is set out from the very start (12:1-3). There Abram, later to be named Abraham, is commanded by God to leave his country of residence and move to a land to be shown to him, where he will become the ancestor of a great and famous nation, specially blessed by God and conferring blessing on other peoples. These first promises are repeated in fuller detail later to Abraham himself (15:4, 7, 18-21; 17:4-8; 22:17-18) and then to Isaac (26:2-5, 24) and Jacob (28:13-15; 35:11-12); but the essentials are already present in 12:1-3. Brevard Childs has pertinently remarked (*Introduction to the Old Testament as Scripture,* 150) that the promises as a whole "relate, above all, to posterity and land." The direction to Abraham to move to a particular country may be taken to imply his future possession of it; the promise that he will become a great nation and that his name will be great equally necessarily implies that he will father an heir and that this fertility will be continued in later generations. The promise of blessing implies their material success; and it is implied quite clearly that God will guide their fortunes in the future. There has been much meticulous academic discussion of the variations in content and form of the different passages in question, which were thought to provide clues regarding the gradual development of the material, but no consensus has been reached. It was part of the literary technique of the biblical writers not only to repeat topics but to adapt their particular expressions to suit their contexts and also to introduce variations into them to relieve monotony and sustain the interest of the readers (Robert Alter, *The Art of Biblical Narrative,* 88-113).

The promise of possession of the land of Canaan, to which Abraham (or his father) had moved from Ur of the Chaldeans (15:7), was in fact never fulfilled in the course of the book of Genesis. The patriarchs are never pictured as owners of the land. The Canaanites (12:6; 13:7) and other peoples (ch. 23) were in possession; Abraham and his family are described as resident aliens (23:4; 35:27), passing through rather than settling. The promises of possession of the land, then, were not for immediate fulfillment but for the future. This is clear from 35:12, where in renewing the promise God says, "the land that I *gave* to Abraham and Isaac I will give to you, and I will give the land to your offspring after you" — when in fact he had *not yet* given possession of the land at all, either to Abraham or to Isaac. The Hebrew verb "give" *(nathan),* here used in a past tense, clearly means something more like "promise to give" in this passage at least.

The promise of the land is expressed in different ways. In 15:7 God tells Abraham "I am Yahweh who brought you from Ur of the Chaldeans, to give you this land to possess." In 15:18, however, the Hebrew phrase used is "to your seed," that is, to Abraham's descendants — Abraham himself is not included here. Elsewhere, in the renewals of the promise to Isaac (26:3) and Jacob (28:13; 35:12) it is "to you and to your descendants (after you)." These differences of phraseology are not, however, really material, as some scholars have argued. In 17:2 it is clear that the promise to Abraham *includes* his descendants by implication, just as "I will make *you* (singular) into a great nation" in 12:2 cannot refer just to one man but must include several generations of his ancestors.

There is then a constant tension and an atmosphere of suspense throughout the patriarchal stories, highlighted also by the final words of the book referring to the burial of Joseph (50:26): "they embalmed him, and he was put in a coffin *in Egypt*" ("in Egypt" being the very last words of the book). The experiences of the patriarchs, despite the promises, have led them merely from one alien land (Ur of the Chaldeans or Haran) to another (Egypt), after four generations of wandering in the land which they hoped to possess but did not yet possess. This postponement of the fulfillment of the promise of the land is further emphasized in God's words to Abraham in 15:13-16, where he predicts that Abraham's descendants will be not only aliens but slaves in a foreign land for four hundred years before settling in Canaan. The author has thus created a dramatic tension between promise and reality, leading the readers to appreciate the precariousness of the existence of the patriarchs and to wonder how and by what means it will come about that their descendants will possess the land — questions which would have a distinct relevance to later Israelites in exile or, somewhat later, forced to live once more in a land which was not theirs. The Exodus from Egypt recounted in the following book would perhaps give them new hope.

The other promises were partly but by no means completely fulfilled within the compass of the book of Genesis. God made a covenant with Abraham and his descendants (15:18; ch. 17) which would remain in force for ever; and he promised to bless them (12:2; 22:17; 26:3; 28:14; 35:11) and to be always with them to guide and prosper them (26:3) until all the promises were fulfilled (28:15). The covenant, the blessing — which implies both material wealth and progeny, and the continuous divine protection — which preserved the existence of the family — may be said to have come into operation immediately. That Abraham and his family became the ancestors of many nations (17:4; 35:11) is also hinted at. But the further promises of becoming a great and famous nation that would be victorious over enemies but also be a blessing to other nations (12:2-3; 17:2-5; 22:17-18; 26:4; 28:14; 35:11) remained yet to be fulfilled.

The ultimate fulfillment of the promise to become a great and numerous nation obviously depended from the start on two things: the survival of the head of the family and his wife (or wives) in each generation, and the successful fathering and bearing, in each generation, of a male heir (Abraham's unenthusiastic proposal to adopt his own servant as his heir is firmly rejected by God: 15:2-4). It is the uncertainty both about survival and about the birth of an heir, apparently despite the promises which God has made, that constitutes the main drama of the patriarchal history. Time and time again these are placed in danger in one way or another, creating a dramatic suspense. Each of these situations is then resolved by God's intervention, often by what we should call a miracle, only to be succeeded by another; so when the reader reaches the end, with Jacob's blessing of his twelve sons who are to become the ancestors of the twelve tribes of Israel, the tension is succeeded by a sense of relief together with confidence in the future. By his ingenuity in combining and adapting a multitude of narrative fragments the author succeeded in creating an epic which held the reader and continues to do so to this day.

The tension begins immediately after Abram's call, with his migration to Egypt in consequence of a famine in Canaan (12:10-20), where the life of Abram and the role of Sarai as the future mother of the heir are endangered. Only Yahweh's intervention in afflicting Pharaoh with plagues, revealing that Sarai is Abram's wife, saves them. The incident results in the beginning of the fulfillment of the promise of blessing, in that Abram emerges as a wealthy man. Then in 13:8-12 the question of the land begins to be settled when Lot chooses the plain of Jordan, leaving Abram the land of Canaan as his place of residence. In ch. 14 Abram's military success over the four kings in order to rescue Lot is probably intended as a foreshadowing of the fulfillment of the promise to become a great nation.

The chapters which follow are concerned with the promise of an heir to Abram and its fulfillment despite serious impediments. The promise is made specifically in 15:4, coupled with the promise of numerous descendants (v. 5). This passage is also significant because it contains one of the few references (v. 6) to Abram's reaction to the promises: he believes them and trusts God to carry them out — an attitude which the author probably wishes to inculcate into a much later Israel in a similar situation of apparent helplessness. This was a remarkable act of faith in view of

Sarai's persistent barrenness (16:1) and advanced years, and also of Abram's own old age (17:17); and God acknowledged this act of faith and gave Abram credit for it (literally, "counted it to him as righteousness"). Ch. 16 tells the story of Hagar and the birth of Ishmael; Abram's ability to bear children is thus demonstrated, but it is not in this way that he is to be granted an heir. He is told by God (17:20-21) that Ishmael, whose mother is Egyptian (16:1), is not to be his heir: the heir is to be the child of both Abraham and Sarah (both now renamed, 17:5, 15). Sarah's infertility is mysteriously overcome, despite her skepticism, by the arrival of three visitors, who announce the miraculous birth (18:1-15). But now once again an impediment occurs. Once again Abraham and Sarah migrate to another country and Sarah is taken into the harem of the Philistine Abimelech, king of Gerar (20:1-18); and once again God intervenes by telling the king that she is Abraham's wife. Finally all this suspense is resolved: at last their son Isaac is born, and the continuation of the family appears to be assured (21:1-7).

Even now, however, a fresh danger appears: Isaac's life is now put in jeopardy, in the most dramatic of all these incidents, and by God himself. Abraham is commanded by God to sacrifice his son Isaac. He obeys, and is at the very point of sacrificing Isaac when the angel of God stops him in the nick of time. Although it is then explained that God's intention was only to test Abraham's *readiness* to sacrifice to God that which he most dearly loved, the story is told brilliantly in a way that creates the maximum suspense.

In the generations that follow the same theme continues to be central. The old problem of ensuring that the family succession should be preserved from foreign taint which had arisen when Ishmael was Abraham's only son is still to the fore. The first problem now to be dealt with, then, was the fear that Isaac might marry a Canaanite wife. Ch. 24 describes how this danger was averted when Abraham's servant was divinely guided to the house of Isaac's cousin Bethuel in Aram-naharaim (in Mesopotamia) and was able to arrange a marriage between Isaac and Bethuel's daughter Rebekah.

In the next generation the succession to the promises was again in doubt. The rivalry between Isaac's twin sons Esau and Jacob led to a threat to kill Jacob (27:41), and Jacob had to flee for his life. At Bethel, where he spent the night while on his journey, it was made plain to Jacob that he and not his elder twin was to inherit the promises made to Abraham and Isaac (28:13-15); and, like his father, he wished to marry his cousin

(Rachel). Nevertheless, Jacob had to pass through a series of dangers — from his father-in-law Laban (ch. 31), from a mysterious adversary who wrestled with him (32:22-32), from Esau (ch. 33), and from the Shechemites whom his sons had offended (ch. 34).

In the story of Joseph (chs. 37-50), which differs in many ways from those of Abraham and Jacob, the same theme of dire threat to the survival of the heirs subsequently miraculously averted by God continues unabated. The central figure in these chapters is Joseph, who as the eleventh son of Jacob was far from being the expected heir; but, as it becomes clear, Joseph's survival proves to be essential for that of his brothers, because it is he who, himself miraculously saved, is to be the savior of *their* lives.

This story begins (ch. 37) with the young Joseph, hated by his brothers, who plot his death. He is saved by the persuasion of his brother Judah, but nevertheless sold to passing Ishmaelites and taken as a slave to Egypt. In chs. 39-41 we follow the ups and downs of Joseph's extraordinary career: sold to Potiphar, the captain of Pharaoh's guard, as a slave (39:1); promoted to overseer of Potiphar's household (v. 6); accused by Potiphar's wife of attempted rape (v. 17) and imprisoned (v. 20); freed from prison and brought to Pharaoh's notice by a fellow prisoner who remembered his ability to interpret dreams (41:9-14); and forthwith promoted to the highest office in the Egyptian state, governing the whole country (41:38-45).

From his position of unlimited power Joseph is instrumental in saving the lives of his father and brothers and all their children and grandchildren from certain starvation by inviting them to migrate from Canaan to Egypt, where alone, thanks to his own efforts, there was plenty of food (45:9–46:27). Later, however (45:5-8; 50:19-20), Joseph specifically attributed his survival and good fortune to God, who was the real controller of all these events and had sent him to Egypt "in order to preserve the lives of many people."

In his dying words (50:24) Joseph reminded his brothers of the promise of the land, not yet achieved: the family had been saved yet again, this time from famine, but their residence in Egypt was not the final stage, not what God intended for them. "I am about to die; but God will surely come to you, and bring you up out of this land to the land that he swore to Abraham, to Isaac, and to Jacob." This theme, then, is never very far from the center of the narrative of Gen. 12-50.

Of the three main patriarchal "histories" — of Abraham, Jacob, and Joseph — it has already been remarked that the account of Abraham is the least integrated. It hardly forms a consecutive "history" at all. Each incident is to a large extent independent and self-contained, and in several — notably the stories of Hagar and Ishmael (chs. 16 and 21) and of Lot at Sodom (ch. 19) — Abraham either does not appear at all or is only a peripheral figure. However, some stories have the character of "set pieces" written to express the "theology" of the author. This is true of the theological discussion in 18:17-33, which has no bearing on the fortunes of Abraham; ch. 22, though now integrated into the main theme of the promises by its relevance to the survival of the heir, is also a theological creation in its present form. A further feature of these chapters is that some of the incidents described could well have been originally told of someone other than Abraham, perhaps even of unnamed persons, in the manner of a legend or even a fairy tale (German *Märchen*). All the stories are short — there is no real continuity except what has been imposed on them by the author.

The history of Jacob is somewhat more integrated. The incidents are on the whole told at greater length, and the adventures of Jacob form a more continuous narrative plot. As has already been noted, two distinct plots have been combined here: that of Jacob and his relations with his brother Esau (25:21–28:22, resumed in chs. 32-33) and that of Jacob and his relations with his uncle Laban (chs. 29-31); but the story is told as part of a single account of Jacob's life. It begins with the births of Jacob and his twin brother Esau and their rivalry, leading to Esau's threat to Jacob's life and to the flight of Jacob, and ends with the return of Jacob and his reconciliation with his brother: a "classic" tale of the unsatisfactory son who made good. The intervening years of Jacob's life are filled with a mixture of good and evil fortune: his marriages and the birth of his children on the one hand and his intolerable servitude to Laban on the other, from which he eventually escapes with his family. The tale is interspersed with incidents which confirm Jacob's position as the heir to the promises. There is thus a kind of jerkiness in the narrative at some points, but Jacob's personality is depicted in a way which is not the case in the history of Abraham. The modern reader at least will find an interest in the depiction of the development of that personality, from that of the brash and tricky young man to that of the responsible patriarch.

When we come to the final section of Genesis, the history of Joseph, we are immediately struck by the fundamental difference between it and the histories of Abraham and Jacob. The Joseph story belongs to a completely different literary genre. Apart from ch. 38, which is completely unrelated to its context and has for some reason been inserted into it, this is a perfectly integrated and fully structured narrative about the life of

Joseph which at least in its present form is the creation of the Pentateuchal author. Von Rad characterizes it as "a novel through and through," though "short story" probably better represents von Rad's meaning ("The Joseph Narrative," 292). It has many of the characteristics which we look for in a novel: unity of plot, suspense, dramatic irony, the depiction of "involved psychological situations" (von Rad), characterization of the hero, changes of tempo to suit particular situations. It is clearly an independent work of literary artistry, a piece of considerable length and not the result of combining a series of shorter stories. At the same time, in its present form and in its present position within the Pentateuch it forms part of the wider history, performing the function of a link between the earlier histories of Abraham's descendants and the next stage — the Exodus from Egypt — skillfully contriving a plausible reason for the presence of the tribal ances-tors in Egypt on which the larger plot depends.

But it also seems evident that the history of Joseph was intended to serve some didactic purpose beyond this. Simply in order to achieve this result it cannot have been necessary to devote fourteen chapters of the present text to such an elaborate story — with its descriptions of Egyptian court life, the administrative problems of the Egyptian economy and their solution, the long, drawn-out account of Joseph's treatment of his brothers when they traveled to Egypt to buy grain, and his interpretation of the dreams of Pharaoh, the butler, and the baker.

Essentially the plot, the story of a young man who through his own ability rises from obscurity to unheard-of power and wealth, is one commonly found in folktales (e.g., Dick Whittington). But it is also an example of a particular Jewish variation of this theme: that of the Jewish captive at the court of the foreign king, who turns the tables on his conquerors and is awarded the highest position in the kingdom. This is also the theme of the stories about Daniel in Dan. 1-6 and of the book of Esther. Joseph and Daniel also have in common their unsurpassed ability to interpret dreams, by means of which they achieve their success, and also their acknowledgment that their success is due not to their own ability but to God. Joseph, then, is presented in these chapters as a hero, but one who gives the credit to God. Once more there is a lesson here for later Jews living in subservience to a foreign conqueror.

Von Rad, who made a special study of these chapters, saw the story as an example of wisdom literature. Joseph, he argued, was the model of the accomplished government administrator or court scribe. He possessed all the virtues which, according to the wisdom teaching both of Egypt and

Israel (the latter exemplified in the book of Proverbs), would lead to success in that profession, especially ability to give good advice at the right moment, modesty, learning, courtesy, and self-control, in addition to the recognition that all success was dependent on the will of God. The Joseph story was influenced by Egyptian models and was one of the literary consequences of the cultural "enlightenment" which Israel derived from Egypt in the reign of Solomon. It was no coincidence, von Rad believed, that the story has been compared with the Egyptian *Tale of the Two Brothers* (*ANET,* 23-25). Its marked interest in foreign, specifically Egyptian, life and customs is also readily explicable in terms of this theory.

Von Rad's thesis was at first widely accepted, but it has recently been subjected to serious criticism. Apart from the widespread rejection of the theory of a "Solomonic enlightenment" and the opinion of competent Egyptologists that the story shows little knowledge of Egypt — and certainly not of the period when von Rad supposed it to have been written — it has been pointed out that its portrait of Joseph does not in fact closely correspond to the scribal ideal. Joseph was not born into a scribal family as would normally have been the case for scribes. Nothing is said of his education; rather, his ability seems to have been innate. It is far from being the case that he was self-controlled: in 45:1-2 he broke down completely and wept so loudly that "the Egyptians heard it, and the household of Pharaoh heard it." Moreover, his telling of his early dreams to his family in ch. 37 reads like arrogance rather than modesty, although it may have been the intention of the author to portray the subsequent development of Joseph's character. There is little doubt that Joseph was intended as a model to be in some way imitated; but it must be doubted that he is represented as a model scribe.

The difference in genre between the story of Joseph and the previous "histories" suggests that, rather than piecing together and rewriting a mass of fairly brief but originally independent pieces and adding a few more of his own, the author has here composed an entirely original story. He has already mentioned the birth of Joseph in the course of the history of Jacob (30:22-24), and Joseph's name occurs again several times in the later part of that history, although nothing further is recorded of him there. Joseph appears again, however, in the blessings of Jacob (49:22-26), which appear to be a kind of delayed epilogue to the history of Jacob; but what is said of him there has nothing at all in common with the character and life of Joseph otherwise depicted in chs. 37-50 except for the statement in 49:26 that he was "set apart from his brothers" (or possibly "was prince over his brothers"). It may be this phrase that the author took as his starting point for his story, though he may have known of a tradition about the migration of Jacob and his family to Egypt.

To conclude, in our discussion of Gen. 12-50 we have seen how the author employed a variety of methods of composition. There is, first of all, reason to suppose that it was he who "created" the family history of the patriarchs. This is made probable by the fact that outside the Pentateuch the extant preexilic literature shows virtually no knowledge of them as individuals or of the events associated with them, although their names sometimes appear as designations of the nation or of particular segments of it. It is probable, therefore, that various stories about legendary persons, perhaps originally attached to particular places or regions of Palestine, have been linked together by the Pentateuchal author by representing these persons as successive generations of a single family which branched out in a fourth generation into the "twelve tribes of Israel," so creating an etiology of the origin of the nation which later became accepted as the national tradition.

This was a considerable achievement. Admittedly the stories of Abraham and Jacob do not read entirely smoothly: in places they remain episodic, and also some inconsistencies remain. There the rewriting may have been little more than retouching, although an impression of continuity — of a "biography" — has been achieved. Some of the longer episodes, however — notably the battle against the kings (ch. 14), the announcement of Isaac's birth and the dialogue between Abraham and God (ch. 18), the story of the near-sacrifice of Isaac (ch. 22), the journey to find a wife for Isaac (ch. 24), and the deception of Isaac (ch. 27) — clearly go beyond the genre of the folktale: they are the work of an accomplished author. This is pre-eminently true of the story of Joseph, where literary imagination was given free rein and the literary art displayed to perfection.

For Further Reading

Blenkinsopp, Joseph. *The Pentateuch: An Introduction to the First Five Books of the Bible.* New York: Doubleday and London: SCM, 1992, ch. 4.

Davies, Philip R. *In Search of "Ancient Israel."* JSOT Supplement 148. Sheffield: JSOT Press, 1992.

Gunkel, Hermann. *The Legends of Genesis.* New York: Schocken, 1964. (Translated from the Introduction to his first [German] commentary on Genesis, 1901.)

McKane, William. *Studies in the Patriarchal Narratives*. Edinburgh: Handsel, 1979.

Moberly, R. W. L. *Genesis 12-50*. OTG. Sheffield: JSOT Press, 1992.

Noth, Martin. *A History of Pentateuchal Traditions*. Englewood Cliffs, N.J.: Prentice-Hall, 1972. Repr. Atlanta: Scholars Press, 1989. (First published in German, 1948.)

von Rad, Gerhard. *Genesis*. 3rd ed. OTL. Philadelphia: Westminster and London: SCM, 1972. (9th German ed., 1972.)

————. "The Joseph Narrative and Ancient Wisdom," in *The Problem of the Hexateuch and Other Essays*. Edinburgh: Oliver & Boyd, 1966, 292-300. Repr. Philadelphia: Fortress and London: SCM, 1984. (First published in German, 1953.)

Redford, Donald B. *A Study of the Biblical Story of Joseph*. VTS 20. Leiden: Brill, 1970.

Rendtorff, Rolf. *The Old Testament: An Introduction*. London: SCM, 1985, and Philadelphia: Fortress, 1986. (First published in German, 1983.)

Van Seters, John. *Abraham in History and Tradition*. New Haven: Yale University Press, 1975.

————. *Prologue to History: The Yahwist as Historian in Genesis*. Louisville: Westminster/John Knox, 1992.

Westermann, Claus. *Genesis 12-36*. Minneapolis: Augsburg and London: SPCK, 1985. (First published in German, 1981.)

————. *Genesis 37-50*. Minneapolis: Augsburg and London: SPCK, 1986. (First published in German, 1982.)

Whybray, R. Norman. *The Making of the Pentateuch*. JSOT Supplement 53. Sheffield: JSOT Press, 1987.

See also other commentaries listed above.

CHAPTER 5

Exodus, Leviticus, Numbers: Narratives

WHEN THE STORY of Abraham's family is resumed at the beginning of the book of Exodus they have become a nation. The first seven verses of the book state that the descendants of the seventy persons who were living as a family in Egypt in the time of Joseph (Gen. 46:26-27; Exod. 1:5) had grown in number in the course of 430 years (Exod. 12:40; 400 years according to Gen. 15:13) to a numerous people who "filled the land" of Egypt, in accordance with the promise made to Abraham of numerous progeny "like the sand of the sea." We are told nothing of what happened during that period, though it is implied that they remained welcome immigrants, yet they continued to live apart from the Egyptians. Exodus, then, marks an entirely new stage in their history; and the author makes this quite clear in that the phrase "the sons of Israel" (i.e., of Jacob) — which in Exod. 1:1 has a literal meaning — has already from v. 7 on acquired the new meaning of "the Israelites."

Exodus, Leviticus, and Numbers belong together: there are no natural divisions between them. The division of the Pentateuch into five books, though ancient, is not original. It is probably due partly to a somewhat rough assessment of their contents and partly to practical considerations which limited the quantity of material that could conveniently be included on a single scroll. Of the five books, only Genesis and Deuteronomy have clearly distinct characters of their own.

These three books carry the story — now the story of the *people* of Israel — from their settled residence in Egypt to "the plains of Moab by the Jordan at Jericho" on the east side of the river (Num. 36:13). There they were poised to enter the Promised Land at last, an event delayed only by a lengthy series of discourses, together with a song and a blessing pronounced by Moses, and by Moses' death — all of which are the subject of Deuteronomy.

The distance between Egypt and Palestine, especially from the region where the Israelites were settled (apparently in the east of the Nile delta not far from the frontier), is not great. These are adjacent territories, and there was in ancient times a good military road which passed through them. Yet we are told that the Israelites took forty years to arrive at their destination! It is stated in Exod. 13:17-18 that God deliberately led them by a roundabout way rather than by way of "the land of the Philistines," which would have been nearer. In Num. 14:26-35; 32:10-13 the reason for the forty years' journey is given: it was God's intention that this should be a punishment for disobedience and rebelliousness committed after the people left Egypt. Forty years is a round figure for a generation, and God intended that during that period none of the men then aged twenty years or more (with the two exceptions of Caleb and Joshua) should be permitted to enter the Promised Land, but that they should all die in the wilderness. Eventually the Israelites entered the land under Joshua, not from the Egyptian side but from the east, through Moab and across the Jordan.

These three books may in fact be divided in terms of location into two main parts. The first fifteen chapters of Exodus are located in Egypt and its environs. They recount the oppression of the Israelites in Egypt, Moses and the plagues, the Exodus itself, and the miraculous crossing of the Sea. The second and longer part is entirely concerned with the journey of Israel through the wilderness. This includes the events at Sinai, which occupy a large section — from Exod. 19 to Num. 10:12 — and the entire book of Leviticus. From the literary point of view, however, these books differ markedly from Genesis in that only about one-third of these 103 chapters can be said to consist of narrative. Most of the rest consists of laws, instructions, and regulations (and in some cases, especially in the account of the tabernacle, their execution) laid down by God through Moses, many of them at Sinai. In many cases, especially in Numbers, law is so intertwined with narrative that it is hardly possible to distinguish one from the other.

These laws will be discussed in more detail in chapter 7 below; but at this point it is relevant to consider the role that they play in their context in Exodus-Numbers and in the Pentateuch as a whole. The context is a narrative one: these are not timeless laws unrelated to the events in the story. They are presented as having been promulgated at particular times and in particular places, so that they are an essential part of the narrative. The reader is made aware of the circumstances in which the basic constitution of the nation was given to it. There is a sense in which everything from Genesis on has been leading up to the Sinai event. It is for this reason that the whole of the Pentateuch — unlike any other book of the Old Testament — is known to the Jews as Torah ("law" or "instruction"). Sinai is the place in the wilderness to which Moses asked and was refused permission by Pharaoh for the people to go to worship their God (Exod. 5:3; 7:16; 8:27) and to which God is referring when he says, "Tell the Israelites: 'You have seen what I did to the Egyptians, and how I bore you on eagles' wings and brought you to myself'" (19:3-4). It is here that the people enter into a covenant with God and promise to obey his laws (19:3-8; 24:3-8; 34:10, 28).

The Figure of Moses

Moses dominates the whole of these three books and Deuteronomy as well. He embodies all the qualities and functions of a leader. Under God's direction he is the one source of authority as ruler and director of the people. He is also, on occasion, a victorious commander in war. He is lawgiver and judge, and performs actions normally associated with the priesthood, although it is his brother Aaron who is said to be a priest. He is also a prophet and a teacher. It is through Moses that God communicates his will to the people. He acts as an intercessor when the people have sinned. He is the mediator of the covenant which God makes with the people, and it is he who, acting always under God's direction, is their savior and protector. Moses is, then, what we should call a hero — the unique hero of his time. Yet he is also supremely a man of God and a servant of God who is himself the object of divine rebukes on several occasions.

It is obvious that this picture of such an all-embracing authority figure cannot be a homogeneous one, incorporating as it does all the functions of rulers and of holy men that later Israel was to encounter during its history. It would seem rather that, whatever historical reality may lie behind this figure, there has been a legendary development, perhaps of tremendous proportions. Every aspect of greatness and virtue has been piled on Moses at some later time, making him an ideal person, the fount and origin of all subsequent nobility and greatness — a development comparable with that concerning David, and to a lesser extent Samuel and Solomon.

That such a development took place is generally acknowledged; it appears to have occurred at a comparatively late date. It is striking that, as with Abraham, Jacob, and Joseph, there are hardly any references to Moses in any of the Old Testament books outside the Pentateuch that can with certainty be regarded as preexilic, and none that shows any knowledge of the events of his life as recounted in the Pentateuch. Only 2 Kgs. 18:4, which may have preserved an older tradition, refers to one such incident, connecting it specifically with Moses' name: his setting up a bronze serpent in the wilderness (Num. 21:4-9). This reference is negative rather than positive; although it does not specifically criticize Moses' action, it regards the bronze serpent itself — which had apparently been preserved and placed in the temple at Jerusalem — as something which had become an object of idolatrous worship and which Hezekiah, in cleansing the temple and restoring the pure worship of Yahweh there, had praiseworthily destroyed. The earliest reference to Moses in the prophetic books is Jer. 15:1, where he is named together with Samuel as a famous intercessor. Moses' name is not so much as mentioned by any of the preexilic prophets.

The view of Moses' importance underwent a complete change in the postexilic period. Some of the postexilic literature (Mal. 4:4; Neh. 9:14; 13:1; Dan. 9:11-13) cites Moses as lawgiver, or refers to his "book" or "law" as binding on Israel; in other texts (Isa. 63:11-12; Mic. 6:4; Pss. 77, 105, 106) there is clearly a familiarity with the Pentateuchal story, with allusions to Moses in connection with such events as the Exodus and the miracle at the Sea and his leadership in the wilderness. His reputation, thus once established, has remained unchanged in Judaism ever since.

It is difficult to account for this transformation. Some scholars have supposed that the original Moses tradition was confined to only one of the various Pentateuchal themes, and that the notion of his connection with the others was a subsequent development. Two themes that have been frequently suggested as his original "location" are the Exodus (together with the miracle at the Sea) and the making of the covenant, along with the giving of the Law at Sinai. Martin Noth saw the origin of the Moses tradition in the "occupation" theme, though he was very skeptical even about this. Even there the original tradition had contained no information about Moses apart from the note regarding his burial (Deut. 34:6) — the only genuine indication that he existed at all! Of the two other proposals, that the oldest Moses tradition is to be found either in the Exodus story or in the Sinai pericope, the latter is perhaps the more plausible view. Several references to him in the postexilic books speak simply of the authoritative "law" or "book" of Moses, whereas in many of the innumerable references to the Exodus or to the miracle at the Sea his name is not mentioned at all.

To what extent it was the author of the present Pentateuch who created the "biography" of Moses is not clear. In view of the methods which he employed in Genesis, it is reasonable to accord him a large part in this. From the literary point of view it is clear that it is the figure of Moses which now holds the story together and gives it a focus. Many of the stories are quite short, and it seems probable that these could have already been circulating in the author's time; not all of them need have been originally connected with Moses himself. But if Moses was already revered as lawgiver, it is not surprising that other great events should have been attributed to him, notably the Exodus, the miracle at the Sea, and the journey toward the Promised Land.

That the story of Moses as recounted in the Pentateuch is a late literary construction is supported by a recent and increasingly accepted hypothesis put forward on other grounds, that there was no mass immigration of Israel into Canaan from outside at all! George E. Mendenhall and Norman K. Gottwald were the first to cast doubt on the historical credibility of the migration from Egypt to Canaan, and on the role of Moses in such a movement. Their view has been supported on both archaeological and sociological grounds. These scholars and those who have followed them maintain that there was no occupation of the land from outside. Rather, the later Israelites were actually descendants of part of the Canaanite population which, whether individually or in a corporate revolutionary movement, had detached itself from the life of the Canaanite cities of the plains with their surrounding agricultural territories, and had gradually established itself in the previously uninhabited, or sparsely inhabited, hill country. There was no "conquest" of Canaan by immigrants, nor was there a gradual infiltration by nomads — the main alternative theories previously dominant. Modern archaeological research has revealed that there was neither a cultural nor a linguistic break which would suggest the arrival of a new population. Mendenhall ("The Hebrew Conquest of Palestine," 73) envisaged

the withdrawal, not physically and geographically, but politically and subjectively, of large population groups from any obligation to the existing political regimes. . . . In other words, there was no statistically important invasion of Palestine. . . . There was no real conquest of Palestine . . . [but] a peasant's revolt against the network of interlocking Canaanite city states.

Subsequent scholars have differed about the causes of such an internal movement of population but have held on to the general theory (e.g., Gottwald, *The Tribes of Yahweh,* 36-41; Niels P. Lemche, *Early Israel,* 411ff.; Giovanni Garbini, *History and Ideology in Ancient Israel,* 64). But if the present Moses story is largely a purely literary creation, a question arises concerning the origin of the religion of Yahweh which the Pentateuch so closely associates with the figure of Moses. Some proponents of the "internal development" hypothesis, though rejecting the notion of a mass immigration, have conceded the possibility that although the origins of the Israelite people as a whole must be looked for on the soil of Palestine, there may have been a small group of people (sometimes known as "the Moses group") who had been slave laborers in Egypt, had made their escape, and had then arrived in Palestine, having both in Egypt and on their journey undergone some experiences associated with a god named Yahweh who had in some way been their deliverer. It was this small group which, having been absorbed into the newly formed people of Israel, had introduced the worship of Yahweh to their new compatriots. Such a theory might account for the fact that some of these traditions seem to have been known, especially to the eighth-century prophet Hosea and his northern audience. But this would not account for a Pentateuchal narrative concerning an army of 600,000 men with their families, augmented by a further "mixed crowd," and accompanied by numerous flocks and herds, who supposedly walked through the desert under the direction of Moses for forty years (Exod. 12:37-38).

Why should the Pentateuchal author have concocted such a story, and why did it eventually come to be so universally accepted by later Jews as the basis of their beliefs about their origin and their relationship to God? It must be remembered that the Pentateuch as we have it now is on any reckoning a document written many centuries after the time when the events that it describes are purported to have occurred. Consequently, unless there were strong oral traditions about that remote era which strongly contradicted the Pentateuchal story, there is no reason why it should have been disbelieved. There may well have previously been little or no such "folk memory." It must further be remembered that the Pentateuch was probably the first comprehensive account of Israelite origins to be written, at about the same time as such works became fashionable in the civilized world. Some Jewish literature of a later period — midrashes, apocalypses, "testaments," and the like — show that many people were ready to believe much more extravagant stories about Israel's origins and early history than this.

Moreover, as has already been noted with regard to Genesis, such a story — of a generation which was so wonderfully saved and protected by its God, yet because of its sin and rebelliousness was in the end denied access to the land which had so long been promised — would convey both a welcome assurance of God's supreme power over the nations of the world and also a warning message to a postexilic generation which did not yet repossess that land, that only if it was obedient could it expect further benefits from its God. If the Pentateuchal story was new to that generation, it was extremely relevant to its situation. That it has been so completely accepted as a true account by countless generations of the Jewish people is a tribute to its literary merit and compelling power.

Moses and the Exodus (Exodus 1-15)

Johannes Pedersen, writing at a time (1934) when much of the Old Testament was thought to be of cultic origin, suggested that these chapters are a unified story based on the "cultic legend" of the Feast of the Passover — that is, an account of the origin of that feast which was solemnly recited at its annual celebration. The core of this theory was, of course, that ch. 12 describes the first celebration of the Passover on the eve of the departure of the Israelites from Egypt.

Although Pedersen's theory has not received a general scholarly assent, and these chapters appear to have been pieced together from many originally independent sources, they have in their present form a strong element of continuity, stronger than in most of the other parts of the total story. Not only is the figure of Moses central to them, but they present a clearly "biographical" appearance. Moses is the principal agent in saving his people from their distress. His birth and early life are described. He then must flee for his life to Midian, but receives a commission from God to return to Egypt and to lead his people away from their oppression there. After an initial reluctance Moses does return and confronts the pharaoh. Pharaoh's initial refusal to let Israel go is overcome by the infliction on

Egypt of a series of plagues sent by God but announced by Moses as his agent, ending with a plague so terrible that the terrified Egyptians assist the Israelites' departure. A further attempt by Pharaoh to retain the service of the Israelites is overcome in a miraculous crossing of the "Sea" by the Israelites, while Pharaoh's army is drowned. We are then told in conclusion that "the people feared the Lord and believed in the Lord *and in his servant Moses*" (Exod. 14:31), and that a song of victory was then sung.

The Birth of Moses

The life stories of famous individuals or heroes often began, in the ancient world and even in more recent times, with an account of mysterious circumstances that surrounded the birth of the hero and in some way presaged the hero's future greatness. Such stories frequently involve supernatural, and even cosmic, happenings. For example, Glendower in Henry IV Part I (3.1) boasted that "the earth did shake when I was born." The story of the birth of Moses (Exod. 2:1-10) is less spectacular, but clearly serves a similar purpose. Born of obscure parents in the tribe of Levi, he was placed in a papyrus basket made watertight with bitumen and placed by his mother in the reeds by the riverbank in an attempt to save him from Pharaoh's threat to kill all the newborn male Hebrew babies. Moses was rescued by Pharaoh's daughter and brought up by her as her son — clearly destined for greatness.

It is of considerable interest to note that a somewhat similar story is told of King Sargon of Agade in a legend preserved in Neo-Assyrian copies (*ANET,* 119). In it the king relates how he was of obscure birth, was placed in the river in a basket made watertight with bitumen, was rescued, and eventually became king. There are striking similarities in the details of the two stories; and although there is no reason to believe that the Pentateuchal author was familiar with the Sargon legend, it is reasonable to suppose that in providing Moses with a birth story he was employing a motif which was well known. The incident presaged the future greatness of one who, though he did not become a king, was to be the ruler of his people. It is rather remarkable that, as in the Sargon legend, there is no mention of divine intervention; but in the context this can be assumed. Like the patriarchs of Genesis, the hero was in danger of death, and from the very moment of his birth; yet he was miraculously preserved.

The account of the birth of Moses should be seen as one of a series of stories about miraculous births. In Genesis, the birth of Abraham's heir Isaac is due to divine intervention which overcomes Sarah's barrenness. The story of the birth of Jacob and Esau presages the divine choice of the younger twin as the heir. In the cases of Isaac and Jacob divine guidance enables them to find their families. With Joseph it is not his birth but his dreams as a young man that presage his future greatness. But again of Moses, Samson (Jgs. 13), and Samuel (1 Sam. 1) there are miraculous birth stories in which a woman's barrenness is overcome — though it is no longer the individual heir to the promises who is involved but other persons whose lives are equally vital to the fate of a nation. Miraculous births may be said to be part of the basic narrative pattern of the Old Testament account of Israel's origins.

The Commissioning of Moses

This account (Exod. 3-6) is prefaced by two stories about Moses as a young man which account for his appearance as a refugee from Egypt in the land of Midian, where he married the daughter of the priest of Midian (2:11-22). These chapters are somewhat confused and contain a number of parallels which cannot be explained by the Documentary Hypothesis of multiple continuous sources. Joseph Blenkinsopp's comment on Exod. 1 is also relevant here: "The compiler . . . doubtless drew on narrative traditions in either written or oral form, but they are not clearly identifiable as segments of continuous sources" (*The Pentateuch*, 145). This is true even of ch. 6, which is usually attributed to P. Despite the inconsistencies in detail, the author's purpose can be clearly seen. This was to give the reader an impression of the very great difficulties faced by Moses in his attempt to carry out the task that God imposed on him, to act as his agent in securing the release of the Israelites from Egypt (3:1-12). The author presents these difficulties one after the other: the problem of convincing Pharaoh of the identity and the power of the God who demanded their release (3:13-17); the reluctance of Pharaoh to release the Israelites and his negative reaction to the request, demanding even greater productivity from them (5:2-14); and the consequent attack on Moses by the Israelite foremen who regarded Moses as a troublemaker whose well-meaning interference had made their situation worse rather than better (5:15-21). This attack provoked a bitter complaint to God by Moses, which in return called forth from God a confirmation of his intention to force Pharaoh's hand. It is noteworthy that this speech by

God in ch. 6 is not, as has often been supposed, a "second call" of Moses parallel with that in ch. 3. It differs significantly from it in that it is a statement of what *God* will do. The burden is shifted from Moses, whose role is now simply to inform the Israelites of what God has promised; but they still remain unconvinced. The scene is now set for the story of the "plagues" and of Pharaoh's stubborn refusal to release the Israelites until his resistance is finally broken (12:29-32).

The Plagues of Egypt

This story (Exod. 7:14–12:32) is a tour de force. Its intention is to demonstrate to the reader that there is no limit to the power of the God of Israel, and that he will exercise that power in whatever way he chooses in defense of his people. Not even the greatest political power in the world — and here Egypt is clearly the symbol of all such power — can withstand God's determination to release Israel from oppression. It is a story that, with its grim humor, would have delighted those who first read it, and who had long suffered from oppression by foreign powers. The protracted series of no less than ten plagues shows that the author had a further purpose beyond that of accounting for their release. Indeed, it would seem obvious that the final plague by itself — the sudden death of all the Egyptian firstborn, including the heir to the throne (12:29-30) — would have been sufficient to bring about Pharaoh's capitulation and make him willingly expel the Israelites, whom (together with their God) he regarded as responsible for this calamity. The multiplication of the number of plagues turns the story into that of a deadly game played against Pharaoh by God. It also enabled the writer to introduce a number of narrative elements which enhanced the narrative and gave it a triumphalist character.

It is important to note that, although at first sight it might seem that it is Pharaoh who plays a game with the Israelites — it is he who time after time frustrates their hopes by first agreeing to let them go and then changing his mind ("hardening his heart") — it is several times made clear (9:12; 10:1-2, 20; 11:10) that it is in fact God who deliberately hardens Pharaoh's heart, so each time provoking yet another plague. This is made absolutely clear in 10:1-2:

> Go to Pharaoh; for I have hardened his heart and the heart of his officials, in order that I may show these signs of mine among them, and

that you may tell your children and grandchildren how I *played a game* [or "toyed"] with the Egyptians, and what signs I have done among them — so that you may know that I am Yahweh.

A more subtle feature of the story concerns the diminishing role played by Pharaoh's court magicians. At first, when Moses and Aaron appear before Pharaoh and Aaron's staff is transformed into a snake, the magicians are able to do the same with their staffs — though Aaron's snake swallows theirs (7:11-12). They are also able to match the first two plagues: the turning of the waters of the Nile to blood (7:22) and the bringing of the plague of frogs (8:7) — though ironically this makes matters worse; they are unable to be really useful and remove the frogs. In 8:18, however, the magicians are unable to turn the dust of the earth into gnats, and exclaim that Moses and Aaron have done this by "the finger of God" (v. 19). Their final appearance is in 9:11, where they are unable to match the plague of boils, and are themselves afflicted by them. After this plague (the sixth) they apparently give up, and disappear from the story.

The ten episodes are recounted with considerable variations within a common basic pattern. Although much is repeated, there are few of the incidents of which it could be said that the same precise model has been adhered to. For example, in a particular case there may or may not be a warning to Pharaoh by Moses before the infliction of a particular plague; the instrument used may or may not be Aaron's staff; the role of Aaron as Moses' companion varies; Yahweh may act directly without reference to any instrument; Pharaoh may or may not appeal to Moses for the plague's withdrawal; there may or may not be a statement that the plague was withdrawn; and so on. The variations in details are almost endless and need not be analyzed in detail. One feature that occurs only in a few cases is the statement that the Israelites, who lived apart from the Egyptians, were not affected by certain plagues. The author presumably intended that this exemption was to be understood as applying to all of them.

Attempts were made by Julius Wellhausen and other documentary critics to account for these variations by distributing the plagues between the sources J (or JE) and P on the basis of distinctive form and content. But in fact they cannot be accounted for by this method; source analysis does not produce neatly consistent results. Each plague story still retains its own particular individuality in the way it is told. Further, the notion that the present text is an amalgam of variant *oral* sources can hardly be maintained; it is difficult to see what motive there could have been for such an operation here. More important, any such methods fail to leave room for the literary imagination of the final author. The action is full of suspense; and yet it moves forward inexorably, as plague follows plague and the disastrous effects of the plagues on the very lives of the Egyptians are intensified, to the final plague and to the climax in the actual departure of Israel from Egypt, so often demanded and so often frustrated. The variations in the telling of the story were, in such an extended narrative, necessary; to describe ten incidents in virtually the same words would have been intolerably dull. The author chose now one, now another detail, while leaving a general impression that what was true of one incident was also true of the others. The result is a masterpiece which would have been ruined by the imposition of complete uniformity.

The plague narrative is strangely interrupted in 12:1-28 by a series of *laws* about the observance of the feasts of Passover and Unleavened Bread, commanded by God to be made known to the people by Moses and Aaron (v. 1 ends with the phrase "in the land of Egypt," as if to give the laws a general rather than a particular setting). Further such laws are given in 12:43-49 and 13:1-16, intermingled with further narrative. The sequence is as follows:

11:4-10:	Announcement of the tenth plague (death of the Egyptian firstborn)
12:1-28:	Passover laws
12:29-32:	The tenth plague
12:33-36:	The Egyptians encourage the departure of the Israelites and load them with gifts
12:37-39:	The Israelites leave Egypt and begin their journey
12:40-42:	Notes on the date of the Exodus and its commemoration by annual keeping of a vigil
12:43-51:	Further Passover laws and their execution
13:1-16:	Further laws on the Feast of Unleavened Bread

The reason for the insertion of these laws into the narrative and the original connection, if any, between the tenth plague and the laws that immediately precede it have been the subject of much discussion. The Pentateuchal author evidently wishes to emphasize the extreme antiquity of divine laws to the greatest possible extent, at times introducing them in a somewhat incongruous manner (e.g., the permission to eat meat provided that the blood was drained from it is traced to the time of Noah;

Gen. 9:3-5), and attributes the particular laws of Israel to the time of Moses; but here he especially presents the laws of Exod. 12 as related to the surrounding narrative (or to some aspects of it). The Passover ritual here prescribed as an annual event (v. 2) is to be a commemoration of what happened on the eve of Israel's departure from Egypt. The details of the ritual are presented as determined by the exigencies of the Israelites' situation: they are to prepare themselves for a hasty flight (v. 11), and to protect themselves from the imminent slaughter of the Egyptians by smearing the blood of the sacrificial Passover lamb on their doorposts (vv. 22-23).

It is such details as these that are at the basis of Pedersen's theory that Exod. 1-15 originated as the "legend" which was recited at the annual celebration of the Passover (see above). For Noth (*A History of Pentateuchal Traditions,* 66) it was the celebration of the Passover itself that had given rise to the development of the plague stories. Others, however, have seen the final plague as an *alternative* to the story of the crossing of the Sea in Exod. 14-15. They have pointed out that there are inconsistencies in the present narrative which are exemplified in ch. 12 with its emphasis on the need for haste and secrecy. According to this view the author has (somewhat ineptly) tried to combine two quite different and mutually inconsistent accounts of the Exodus: one which represents it as a secret flight which Pharaoh, when he became aware of it, tried to thwart by pursuing the fugitives (14:5-9), and one which represents it as an ordered and public departure for which Pharaoh had reluctantly given permission after the slaughter of the Egyptian firstborn (12:31-36). The latter account did not contain, and had no need for, the miracle at the Sea (see George W. Coats, *Moses,* 91ff.). The true climax of the plague stories was not a demonstration of God's power at the Sea but the demonstration of his power in the death of the firstborn and the consequent release of the Israelites.

The Miracle at the Sea

These chapters (Exod. 14:1–15:21) comprise three main sections. Ch. 14 tells, in prose, of the Egyptians' pursuit of the Israelites, the miraculous parting of the waters of the Sea at the stretching out of Moses' hand, the waters' being driven back by a strong east wind so that the Sea is turned into dry land, the Israelites' crossing on dry ground, and the drowning of the Egyptian army by the waters' return to their normal state. Exod. 15:1-18 is a victory song then sung by Moses together with the Israelites, praising Yahweh for their miraculous deliverance but ending (vv. 13-18) with references to subsequent events: the continuing guidance and protection of the people through the wilderness toward the Promised Land; the terror of the Philistines, Edomites, Moabites, and Canaanites at the Israelites' approach; Israel's establishment in the land of Canaan; and finally the building of the temple in Jerusalem. The third, brief component of the chapter is a short victory song sung by Miriam, Moses' sister, to the accompaniment of tambourines (15:20-21).

That there are discrepancies between ch. 14 and the poem in 15:1-18 is hardly surprising, since ch. 15 is clearly not intended to be a literal *account* of the events but is a *hymn of victory* — a type of literature in which factual precision is not called for or expected. In ch. 14 also there are some discrepancies. Neither the cause of the drying up of the sea — a strong east wind or the stretching out of Moses' hand — nor the precise sequence of events is made clear; it has been supposed that the author has here combined two separate versions. In essentials, however, the two chapters agree. The Song of Miriam in 15:21 is a second, very brief, victory hymn which is virtually identical with 15:1b and which, if it immediately followed the Song of Moses, would form a convincing conclusion to that song (compare Pss. 8 and 103 for a similar arrangement). This is the first mention of Miriam (but see Exod. 2:4) and was no doubt introduced here in preparation for the numerous references to her in the book of Numbers.

It has been maintained by some scholars (William F. Albright; Frank M. Cross and David Noel Freedman, *Studies in Ancient Yahwistic Poetry*) that the Song of Moses or Song of the Sea in Exod. 15:1-18 is very ancient, perhaps as old as the twelfth century B.C. Its poetic style and language have been held to be very close to those of Ugaritic poetry. These arguments, however, have been disputed. It is also clear that the attempts by these scholars to interpret vv. 13-18 — which ostensibly refer to later events including the building of Solomon's temple — in quite other ways must be regarded as tendentious.

What is clear is that the Song has been influenced by a myth found in early Canaanite (Ugaritic) and, in other forms, in Mesopotamian literature, namely, what has been called the myth of "God's conflict with the dragon and the sea" — a myth associated in Mesopotamia (but not, as far as our evidence goes, in Canaan) with the creation of the world. This ancient myth has left traces not only in early Israelite literature but in Old Testament literature of all periods, including the book of Daniel (second century B.C.), in literature of the intertestamental period, and even quite clearly in the New Testament (Revelation). Of Exod. 15 John Day writes: "it is very clear that the description has been shaped and influenced by motifs deriving from the myth of the divine conflict with the waters. Thus, the motif of the victory at the sea is associated with Yahweh's eternal kingship" (*God's Conflict with the Dragon and the Sea*, 98). That is to say, the Song is an example of the "historicization of myth" — a mythical motif has been transformed into a supposedly "historical" event. A similar process is reflected in Isa. 51:9-10. Exod. 15, then, cannot have been written before the time of Solomon and may be much later.

What is the location of the "sea" or "Sea" in question? There has been much discussion of this problem. It is important to understand what the question means. Does it mean "Where did these events take place?" or rather "Where did the author(s) present them as having taken place?" As has already been noted, these chapters can hardly be considered as strictly historical accounts; and thus the first of these questions is beside the point. Nevertheless the author has given the story an apparently precise geographical setting, and there is therefore some point in the second question: where did he *imagine* the events to have occurred? But this question is also unanswerable. Martin Noth's comment, after many attempts to answer that issue, remains true: "unfortunately we can no longer make out" where the author located it — "that is if he had any idea at all about geographical relationships in a neighbourhood far removed from the later habitations of Israel" (*Exodus*, 107-8). The only things of which we may be certain are that the author placed it not on the direct coastal route (which he anachronistically called "the way of the Philistines"), since he states that God deliberately guided the people away from this into the wilderness further south (13:17-18), and that the sea in question was not the Red Sea, as the Hebrew *yam-suph* (13:18; 15:4, 22) was rendered in earlier translations. The Hebrew means "sea of reeds," a place whose location is unknown. Similar questions arise with regard to other places recorded as located on the route taken by the Israelites, including Sinai.

The Journey through the Wilderness

The account recorded in Exod. 12:37–Num. 36 lacks the cohesiveness of earlier chapters (of Numbers, Rolf Rendtorff wrote, "Of all the books in the Pentateuch, the book of Numbers is the hardest to survey"; *The Old*

Testament, 146). These chapters comprise several different kinds of material: itineraries, narratives, laws, and institutional matters such as the taking of a census of the tribes. Although they have a narrative framework that forms a bridge between Israel's experiences in Egypt and its entry into the Promised Land, there is no continuous narrative at all. The narrative sections consist mainly of short incidents most of which, though given specific (generally not identifiable) locations, are quite isolated in the sense that they do not form a coherent block but are interspersed with other types of material. It is not surprising that Noth regarded the theme "guidance in the wilderness" (excluding the events at Sinai) as "not a very important or really independent theme" which "presupposes in every instance the themes 'guidance out of Egypt' and 'guidance into the promised land' and depends on both of these," and that "probably this theme arose simply from the narrative desire to tell something concrete about the further fortunes of the Israelite tribes after the 'guidance out of Egypt'" (*A History of Pentateuchal Traditions,* 58, 59).

Nevertheless, the author had some quite specific purposes in composing these chapters. This part of his story afforded him a particular opportunity to make some essential points of a theological nature. Here was a people in transition — not only literally, between Egypt and Canaan, but spiritually. Israel was hardly yet a nation at the beginning of Exodus; by the end of Numbers its character had developed, though scarcely for the better, despite the events at Sinai.

Both God and the people are represented in a fascinating series of incidents as though making one another's acquaintance: testing one another. The word "test, try" (Hebrew *nissah*) is used in these incidents in two distinct ways: *God* tests the people to see whether they will obey him or not (Exod. 15:25; 20:20), and the *people* test *God* to see whether or not he will in fact provide for their material needs in the wilderness (17:2, 7) and to see to what extent he will suffer their disobedience (Num. 14:22). The many instances of their discontent, lack of faith, and rebelliousness against Moses or against God himself (Exod. 14:10-14, immediately after their departure from Egypt; Exod. 16; 17:1-7; 32:1–33:6; Num. 11; 12; 13-14; 16; 20:1-13) reveal a constant change of mood in the three participants, God, Moses, and the people. God is shown as generous and forgiving up to a certain point, but also as angrily punishing rebels with death. At other moments (Exod. 33:3; Num. 14:20-23) he sets limits to his promise to lead the people into the Promised Land. In some cases (Exod. 32:27-34; Num. 12:13-15; 14:13-20; 16:41-50) God shows himself to be capable of changing his mind, and allows himself to be persuaded when Moses appeals for mercy for the rebels.

The relations between God and Moses are equally varied. Moses throughout is God's spokesman, communicating God's words to the people. He also frequently engages in direct dialogue with God. It is he to whom God speaks face to face (Exod. 33:11), and to whom God shows his glory (vv. 18-23). But the texts also speak of Moses' frustration. He complains to God of the intolerable burden of leadership which God had imposed on him, and despairs of his ability to control the people (Exod. 17:4). In a flash of temper he smashes the tablets of the covenant that God had given him (Exod. 32:19). Moses complains of God's treatment of him, and says that he would rather die than carry on (Num. 11:11-15). In Num. 20:11-12 he falls under God's displeasure for losing his temper and is told that he will not be permitted to enter the Promised Land and attain the goal to which his whole life has been devoted.

The depiction of the people is also complex, but mainly negative. At Sinai they appear to be awed by the tremendous events there, and repeat the refrain, "Everything that the Lord has spoken we will do" (Exod. 19:8; 24:3). But in fact the story is of almost constant rebellion by all or part of the people for various reasons. They, like Moses, are condemned to die without reaching the Promised Land — but large numbers of the rebels have already been destroyed by plague, the sword, and other divinely ordained means. The first incidents of rebellion begin immediately after the deliverance of the people at the Sea; already at Sinai the idolatry of the Golden Calf occurs at the foot of the mountain itself (Exod. 32). Toward the end of the narrative (Num. 25) the people practice mass idolatry and sacrifice to other gods at Baal-peor. The author evidently intended to make it quite clear that the people of Israel were entirely unworthy to enter the Promised Land — that they totally ignored the laws which God has imposed on them and that they had promised to keep, and that they totally failed to appreciate what God had done for them in saving them from the Egyptians and guiding them through the wilderness. There could hardly be a clearer lesson for later readers who were living in exile or deprived of actual possession of the land.

The stories about rebellion in the wilderness are quite varied. Some have been derived from popular legends about desert life known to the author. The desert was then, and remains, on the edge of the cultivated land of Palestine with its towns and villages; and its dangers to travelers, especially of death from hunger and thirst, would have been generally known to the inhabitants of the land at any period. The author has used this material, brought it into connection with the person of Moses that he has constructed, and put his own stamp on it. Much of it is his own creation, and in some cases he has used a story more than once in slightly different versions. The main themes on which he lays emphasis are the desire of the people to return to Egypt (where, as they thought and as desert travelers would naturally suppose, they would at least be free from hunger and thirst even though in the immediate past they had lacked freedom); rebellion against Moses; and, to crown all, apostasy from the God who had delivered them.

The incidents concerned with lack of food and water and with the miraculous provision of sustenance (water, Exod. 15:22-25; 17:1-7; Num. 20:2ff.; food, Exod. 16:1ff.; Num. 11) probably have their basis in travelers' tales and may be compared with that of the miraculous feeding of Elijah (1 Kgs. 17:1-6; 19:5-8) or with Elisha's purification of the spring water (2 Kgs. 2:19-22). The names of the places where these events are stated to have occurred — especially Meribah, "strife"; Massah, "testing" — may have given rise to the stories; with regard to the "strife" in particular we may compare the references to quarrels over the possession of springs of water in the desert mentioned in Gen. 13:8; 21:25; 26:19-22. The motif of rebellion against Moses' leadership which occurs in almost all these stories including Exod. 32 (the Golden Calf) and Num. 16 (Korah, Dathan, and Abiram) probably reflects leadership disputes in the postexilic period. Num. 16; Exod. 32; and also Num. 12 (the rebellion of Miriam and Aaron against Moses) are principally concerned with questions of true and false worship and false claims to the priesthood which were certainly living issues at that time.

From Num. 20 on the narrative begins to speak of attempts made by the Israelites to enter the Promised Land. Since God had previously ordained that they should not go by the shortest route, through the (anachronistic) "land of the Philistines" (Exod. 13:17-18), to enter the country from the southeast, the author sends them round via the south to be ready to invade from the west, across the Jordan.

The theological lessons of these narratives are already set out in Num. 13-14. Moses sends a reconnaissance patrol from the wilderness of Paran south of Canaan to report on the fertility of the land and to estimate the military strength of the Canaanites, but they report that an attempt to invade would result in failure and defeat. This news causes a rebellion against the leadership of Moses and Aaron: the rebels propose to choose a new leader and to return to Egypt. An attempt by Caleb and Joshua to persuade the people that victory would be assured if Yahweh were on their side is met with strong hostility, and this arouses the anger of Yahweh, who declares his intention to destroy the whole people and to make Moses the nucleus of an entirely new people. Moses pleads for their forgiveness on the grounds that such an action would lead the Egyptians and Canaanites to conclude that Yahweh was unable to fulfill his promise to give the land to the Israelites. His plea for forgiveness succeeds, although God condemns the whole present generation to die in the wilderness without entering the Promised Land. Only those who had caused the rebellion by bringing back an unfavorable report from their reconnaissance are immediately punished with death by plague. Finally, when the people attempt to invade and conquer the land in defiance of the divine decision, they suffer a humiliating defeat, because God is not with them (Num. 14:40-45).

The lessons of these chapters are twofold — on the one hand, Yahweh's commitment to his promises, the dependence of Israel's success on his goodwill, and his support of his designated leaders; and on the other hand, Israel's lack of faith and unworthiness of Yahweh's blessing, Yahweh's intolerance of disobedience, and his readiness to annihilate the disobedient (which can, however, sometimes be mitigated by the intercession of those who were possessed of his favor). These lessons would not have been lost on the later Israelite readers: only by faith in God's goodwill, by obedience to his chosen leaders, and by rejection of false leaders could they regain possession of the land that they had lost. These lessons are exemplified in the narratives that follow, which are a curious mixture of the positive and the negative: Israel's frustration at the refusal of the king of Edom to let them pass through his land (Num. 20:14-21), an incident which significantly occurs immediately after Moses' and Aaron's demonstration of a lack of trust in God (20:12); the victory over the Canaanite king of Arad (21:1-3); the victories over the Amorites and the king of Bashan, leading to the conquest of their territories (21:21-35); the story of the seer Balaam, who was sent for by Balak king of Moab to curse Israel but found that he could do no other than bless them, since Yahweh had blessed them (chs. 22-24); and then, quite suddenly, Israel's total fall from grace: the intercourse with Moabite women and the consequent worship of their gods, especially Baal of Peor (ch. 25).

The final episodes in this series emphasize the two contrasting yet not incompatible aspects of Israel's situation in the wilderness. On the one

81

hand, by commissioning Joshua as Moses' successor — though he was to act only in accordance with the instruction of the priest Eleazar, who would communicate God's decisions to him (Num. 27:16-23) — God reaffirms his commitment to his promise to give Israel the land of Canaan. On the other hand, it is repeated yet again that only the new generation of young Israelites would be allowed to enter that land and take possession of it (Num. 26:64-65).

Finally, these books have been given a kind of narrative continuity by means of the use of names of places where the various incidents occurred, and by an apparently comprehensive itinerary from Ramses in Egypt to the plains of Moab in Num. 33:1-49 — an itinerary comprising more than fifty place names. The places named in the main narrative as the sites of particular incidents are of course far fewer, but almost all of them appear in the longer list. Many of the names are otherwise unknown, and some may be entirely fictitious. It is also possible that the author used actual routes. Noth suggested that some of the places mentioned may have been stations on a well-known pilgrimage route from Canaan to Sinai (see also Graham I. Davies, *The Way of the Wilderness;* and Philip J. Budd, *Numbers*), and there are other possibilities such as caravan routes, not confined to any particular period.

It is difficult to avoid the impression that these itineraries have been inserted in order to give an impression of historical reality to "an otherwise bald and unconvincing narrative" made up of a mass of originally unconnected items. However this may be, the author has succeeded in giving an impression of Israel as a homeless people constantly on the march — a continuation, in fact, of the situation of the equally homeless and itinerant Abraham and his family in Genesis. The need for a settled existence as promised to the patriarchs and its constant postponement, largely due to the people's sins and lack of faith, were pertinent themes for a later Israel.

For Further Reading

Blenkinsopp, Joseph. *The Pentateuch: An Introduction to the First Five Books of the Bible.* New York: Doubleday and London: SCM, 1992, chs. 5 and 6.

Budd, Philip J. *Numbers.* WBC 5. Waco: Word, 1984.

Childs, Brevard S. *The Book of Exodus.* OTL. Philadelphia: Westminster and London: SCM, 1974.

————. "A Traditio-historical Study of the Reed Sea Tradition," *VT* 20 (1970): 406-418.

Coats, George W. "History and Theology in the Sea Tradition," in *The Moses Tradition*. JSOT Supplement 161. Sheffield: JSOT Press, 1993, 45-56.

————. *Moses: Heroic Man, Man of God*. JSOT Supplement 57. Sheffield: JSOT Press, 1988.

————. *Rebellion in the Wilderness: The Murmuring Motif in the Wilderness Traditions of the Old Testament*. Nashville: Abingdon, 1968.

————. "The Song of the Sea," *CBQ* 31 (1969): 1-17.

————. "The Traditio-historical Character of the Reed Sea Motif," *VT* 17 (1967): 253-265.

Cross, Frank M., Jr. *Canaanite Myth and Hebrew Epic*. Cambridge, Mass.: Harvard University Press, 1973, 112-144.

————, and Freedman, David Noel. *Studies in Ancient Yahwistic Poetry*. SBL Dissertation 21. Missoula: Scholars Press, 1975, 45-65. (Diss., Johns Hopkins University, 1950.)

Davies, Graham I. *The Way of the Wilderness: A Geographical Study of the Wilderness Itineraries in the Old Testament*. Cambridge: Cambridge University Press, 1979.

Day, John. *God's Conflict with the Dragon and the Sea: Echoes of a Canaanite Myth in the Old Testament*. Cambridge: Cambridge University Press, 1985.

Driver, Samuel R. *Introduction to the Literature of the Old Testament*. 8th ed. Edinburgh: T. & T. Clark, 1909.

Garbini, Giovanni. *History and Ideology in Ancient Israel*. New York: Crossroad and London: SCM, 1988. (First published in Italian, 1986.)

Gottwald, Norman K. *The Tribes of Yahweh*. Maryknoll, N.Y.: Orbis, 1979, and London: SCM, 1980.

Johnstone, William. *Exodus*. OTG. Sheffield: JSOT Press, 1990.

Lemche, Niels P. *Early Israel*. VTS 37. Leiden: Brill, 1985.

Mendenhall, Goerge E. "The Hebrew Conquest of Palestine," *BA* 25 (1962): 66-87. Repr. in *The BA Reader* 3, ed. E. F. Campbell, Jr., and David Noel Freedman. Garden City: Doubleday, 1970, 100-120.

Noth, Martin. *Exodus*. OTL. Philadelphia: Westminster and London: SCM, 1962. (First published in German, 1959.)

————. *A History of Pentateuchal Traditions*. Englewood Cliffs, N.J.: Prentice-Hall, 1972. Repr. Atlanta: Scholars Press, 1989. (First published in German, 1948.)

————. *Numbers.* OTL. Philadelphia: Westminster and London: SCM, 1968. (First published in German, 1966.)

Pedersen, Johannes. "The Crossing of the Reed Sea and the Paschal Legend," in *Israel: Its Life and Culture, III-IV.* London: Oxford University Press and Copenhagen: Branner, 1940, 728-737. (First published in Danish, 1934.)

Rendtorff, Rolf. *The Old Testament: An Introduction.* London: SCM, 1985, and Philadelphia: Fortress, 1986. (First published in German, 1983.)

————. *The Problem of the Process of Transmission in the Pentateuch.* JSOT Supplement 89. Sheffield: JSOT Press, 1990. (First published in German, 1977.)

CHAPTER 6

The Book of Deuteronomy

A S HAS BEEN indicated earlier in this book, Deuteronomy occupies a somewhat equivocal status in the Pentateuch. In the Jewish tradition it is the fifth and final book of the Torah, which is the first and most important of the three divisions of the Hebrew Scriptures. In subject matter it is closely related to Exodus-Numbers, being wholly concerned with Moses, and its final chapter (Deut. 34) concludes the history of Moses begun in Exod. 2. However, the view of Martin Noth that Deuteronomy was not originally connected with Exodus-Numbers but is, on the contrary, the first part of another work, a "Deuteronomistic History" — a history of Israel written during the Babylonian Exile and including the books of Joshua, Judges, Samuel, and Kings — has been very widely accepted.

Since W. M. L. de Wette (1806; see chapter 2 above) it has been generally accepted that the "book of the law" whose discovery in the temple during the reign of Josiah (622 B.C.) is recorded in 2 Kgs. 22:8-10 was identical with Deuteronomy or at least with an early version of it. Despite some recent reservations about the historical reliability of the account of Josiah's cultic reform in 2 Kgs. 22-23 (and the somewhat different account in 2 Chr. 34), this view has not been abandoned. Accordingly, Rolf Rendtorff (*The Old Testament*, 155) claims that "the measures taken in Josiah's reform as reported in II Kings 23 show striking affinity to the demands of Deuteronomy. So the connection is indisputable."

Questions of Date and Provenance

Both the date(s) of composition of Deuteronomy and its provenance are disputed. The account in 2 Kgs. 22 gives no indication of the origin or contents of the "book of the law," except that it was believed to be both ancient and authoritative and strongly condemnatory of current cultic practice in Jerusalem. Josiah was appalled by its contents, exclaiming, "Great is the wrath of Yahweh that is kindled against us, because our ancestors did not obey the words of this book" (2 Kgs. 22:13). He consulted the prophetess Huldah, who thereupon delivered an oracle from Yahweh that owing to this disobedience he would bring disaster "on this place and on its inhabitants" in accordance with the penalties set out in the book itself (vv. 16-17). The cultic reform was the consequence. That many of the laws in the book were indeed much older than Josiah's time was argued by a number of scholars. Adam C. Welch, for example, suggested that the laws in the book had originated in northern Israel in the time of Samuel. Others, however, such as Gustav Hölscher, argued for a postexilic date. Some recent scholars favor a date shortly before the discovery of the book, possibly the reign of one of Josiah's immediate predecessors, Hezekiah or Manasseh.

However, it is now recognized that, whatever relationship it may have to Josiah's reform, Deuteronomy is neither the work of a single person nor of a single period. It contains material of very different kinds. Its major and central section is a collection of laws (Deut. 12-26), many of which are closely related to the laws in Exod. 20-23, while others are peculiar to Deuteronomy or differ considerably in detail from those in other collections. The whole collection thus has its own distinctive character.

The first part of Deuteronomy (chs. 1-11) is presented, as is the whole book, in the form of speeches placed in the mouth of Moses addressed to "all Israel beyond the Jordan in the wilderness" on the plains of Moab, and is clearly designed as an introduction to the laws that follow. It begins with a recapitulation of past events: Israel's journey from Sinai (here called Horeb) to the plains of Moab, with emphasis on both God's guidance and the people's apostasy (chs. 1-3). The following chapters, which contain among other things the Ten Commandments (5:6-21) in a slightly different version from that in Exod. 20:1-17, convey solemn warnings to the people to recognize God's goodness in the past and to obey him on their entry into the land, which is imminent. Here also there are reminders of past rebelliousness and warnings of the disastrous con-

86

sequences of further disobedience. These chapters frequently look forward to the laws that follow from Deut. 12:1. Various stylistic features including a series of new introductory formulae at 4:1, 44; 5:1; 6:1, 4; 8:1; 9:1 show clearly that, although in general both style and language remain constant, chs. 1-11 are not a unitary composition.

The third part of the book (chs. 27-34) contains a mixture of material, including lists of blessings and curses giving warning of the consequences of future obedience and disobedience respectively (chs. 27-28), the making of a new and additional covenant (ch. 29), the writing down of the laws of the covenant in a book, together with a command that they are to be read publicly every seven years at the Feast of Booths (31:9-13, 24-26), a song sung by Moses (ch. 32), a blessing pronounced by Moses on the tribes (ch. 33), and finally an account of Moses' death and an assessment of his achievements and character (ch. 34).

It has been pointed out (Dennis J. McCarthy; George E. Mendenhall, "Covenant Forms in Israelite Tradition") that the book as a whole has structural affinities with ancient Near Eastern treaties or formal agreements defining relationships between vassal kingdoms and their imperial masters. In these, the vassals undertook to remain faithful to their overlords in return for their protection. It may be supposed that similar treaties will have been made between some Israelite kings and their Assyrian or Babylonian overlords. Vassal treaties differed from one another in details, but they frequently comprised the following items: a "historical" introduction which stressed past benefits supposedly conferred on the vassal kingdom by its overlords; "stipulations" or conditions which the vassal promised to observe; arrangements for the sealing or ratification of the treaty and its public proclamation; threats or curses to be carried out in case of disobedience; promises of protection by the overlord; and a list of deities cited as having witnessed the making of the treaty.

Although Deuteronomy is not to be regarded as a treaty document in itself, there are remarkable similarities between its structure and that of the extant vassal treaties. Deuteronomy, it has been argued, should be understood as setting out the relationship of the "vassal" Israel, not with a human overlord but with its God, Yahweh. Its opening chapters describe the past benefits conferred by Yahweh on his people. The laws that follow detail the conditions of the relationship, to which obedience is required. Blessings and curses and an account of the making of the covenant, together with its ratification, follow. Although there is nothing in the extant treaties that corresponds to Deut. 30-34, it seems probable that in

Deuteronomy we have the earliest comprehensive theological statement about the relationship between Yahweh and Israel, and that the notion of the vassal treaty, here called a "covenant" (Hebrew *berith*), has played some part in the development of this theology. A further fact linking the two kinds of document is that there are clear affinities between the two types not only in structure but also in style and "technical" language.

Gerhard von Rad ("The Form-Critical Problem of the Hexateuch," 26ff.) argued that the nucleus of the laws in Deuteronomy could be traced back to an early covenant ceremony performed at the Feast of Booths at Shechem. Deut. 27 stipulates that the Israelite tribes, after crossing the Jordan, are to proceed first to the mountains Ebal and Gerizim, which are in the vicinity of Shechem, to set up large stones there on which are to be written down "the words of this law," to build an altar, and to offer sacrifices on it. Other passages such as Deut. 11:29-30; Josh. 8:30ff.; Josh. 24 confirm this connection with Shechem.

But whatever may have been the origin of the laws in this book, Deuteronomy as a whole in its final form bears the marks of a number of subsequent influences. Various theories have been put forward about the nature of the circles in which it may have been composed; each of these has considerable plausibility, yet none of them accounts adequately for all the major features of the book. It must therefore be concluded that the book of Deuteronomy is the product both of widely different periods and also of a variety of authors who represented different and not entirely compatible theological positions. As suggested above, there is a cultic background: the promulgation of the laws is closely associated with ceremonies of oath-taking and the like. There are also a number of laws regulating the membership and status of the priestly class and the conduct of worship, notably the law prohibiting sacrifice at more that one altar (Deut. 12). There is no certainty, however, about the degree of antiquity of this cultic feature.

Another suggested background for Deuteronomy is prophecy. Ernest W. Nicholson in particular *(Deuteronomy and Tradition)* pointed out resemblances between its teaching and that of northern prophets, notably Hosea. These resemblances are to be regarded as indications of a northern provenance of parts of the book, though the teaching in question may have become more widely accepted before its eventual adoption in Deuteronomy. But it is difficult to relate the book's few specific references to prophets with the prophets with whom we are familiar from the prophetic books of the Old Testament (this is also true of the Deuteronomistic

History). There are only three passages which refer specifically to prophets: Deut. 13:1-5; 18:15-22; and 34:10. In 13:1-5 prophets are put on a level with other kinds of person who falsely claim to predict the future by means of dreams and other forms of divination, and who may incite the people. to worship other gods. Deut. 18:15-22, however, distinguishes between prophets who speak in Yahweh's name and those who either speak in the name of other gods or pretend falsely to speak in Yahweh's name. But on a quite different level again it is Moses himself who in 18:15 and 34:10 is designated as a prophet — the only prophet who is named in the book. None of these attitudes toward prophets strikingly recalls the personae of the "classical" prophets, although there are resemblances to oracles in Jeremiah about false prophets.

Von Rad (*Studies in Deuteronomy*, 66ff.), noting the homiletic or sermonlike character of the book, especially chs. 1-11, suggested that it is the work of Levites, living not in Jerusalem but in the country towns, who addressed the people, attempting to persuade them of the importance of Josiah's reform. A variation of this theory by C. Johannes Lindblom saw the authors as northern Levites who had come to live in Jerusalem as a consequence of the reform (2 Kgs. 23:8-9). It was they who brought with them the ancient northern traditions and promulgated them; and they were also responsible for the fierce nationalistic and militaristic tone which appears in the book. Although the Levites are represented as instructing the people in several passages in Deuteronomy (17:9-11; 24:8; 33:10) and in very late texts (2 Chr. 17:9; Neh. 8:9), the wide homiletic function ascribed to them by von Rad and others is based on an assumption which falls considerably short of proof.

Most recently Moshe Weinfeld (*Deuteronomy and the Deuteronomic School*) has advanced the theory that Deuteronomy is the work of scribes in the service of the Judean royal establishment, and that the book is suggestive of wisdom teaching, which was part of the scribes' stock-in-trade. This proposal raises difficult questions about the nature of "wisdom" and its connection with the royal court that cannot be discussed here. The words "wise" (*hakham*) and "wisdom" (*hokhmah*) occur only rarely in Deuteronomy. Still, there are three passages that are significant for Weinfeld's theory. Deut. 4:5-8 extols wisdom as a most desirable and important human quality, and sees it as exemplified in its highest degree in the laws that Yahweh is about to teach to Israel. If Israel obeys those laws, this will cause the other nations to express admiration of Israel as a supremely wise people. According to 1:13-15, wisdom is an essential characteristic of those chosen to be leaders in the affairs of the nation; and 34:9 states that Joshua, Moses' successor, was "full of the spirit of wisdom, because Moses had laid his hands on him."

Deuteronomy certainly shares with the wisdom books of the Old Testament the character of a *teaching* book. In this character it employs vocabulary and phraseology which correspond to that used in Proverbs; but both the context and the contents of the two books differ greatly. Whereas in Proverbs a "father" gives individual instruction to his "son," and that teaching is concerned with the importance of adopting "wisdom" (not with any legal overtones) as a means to personal success in life, what is to be taught to the children in Deuteronomy — and on a national scale — is a knowledge of the laws contained in the book (Deut. 6:20-25). The consequence of failure to learn and obey these is primarily a national, not an individual, calamity.

Apart from a common emphasis on the importance of the teaching, the contents of the two books differ in almost every respect. Deuteronomy is fiercely nationalistic; Proverbs never mentions Israel at all nor appears to be concerned with nations as such. Deuteronomy is much concerned with the elimination of idolatry; Proverbs never mentions any worship but that of Yahweh. Deuteronomy is concerned with public worship and its character; Proverbs rarely mentions this. The list of differences could be extended. It is true that there are laws in Deuteronomy which correspond closely to passages in the wisdom literature, for example, laws against the removal of boundary stones (Deut. 19:14; Prov. 22:28; 23:10), against the use of false weights and measures (Deut. 25:13-16; Prov. 11:1; 20:23), and on making vows (Deut. 23:21-23; Prov. 20:25; Eccles. 5:1-6). But such matters are not confined to the wisdom literature: they were matters of general acceptance. More weight should perhaps be attached to Weinfeld's other major contention that the international treaty form which influenced the composition of Deuteronomy would be particularly well known to government scribes; but in fact the form may have been more widely known, since many of the extant vassal treaties carry a stipulation that they should be regularly read publicly in the vassal country, a practice with which Judah would have been only too familiar in the latter half of its monarchic period.

The Theology of Deuteronomy

Deuteronomy is then probably to be seen as a deliberate amalgam, formed from many diverse elements of the traditional faith of Israel. It must therefore, in its final form, be a relatively late book. It has a unique status not only in the Pentateuch but also in the Old Testament. In the hands of the final editors it presents a complete, more or less coherent theology — the only fully conceived theology in the Old Testament, and one which was to have a profound influence on subsequent thought, as may be seen especially in the Deuteronomistic History and in the final editions of several of the prophetic books. The "Deuteronomic" theological movement, which may have begun as early as the religious reform carried out by Hezekiah (2 Kgs. 18:3-4), marked a new beginning in the history of Israelite religion. The editors of Deuteronomy represented this theology as if it were the original true religion inaugurated by Moses. However, there can be no doubt that the book is the result of an intensive theological thought superimposed on a much less systematically organized Israelite religion which — whether Yahwistic or largely polytheistic in character — had been mainly lacking in systematic reflection.

In its teaching about God, Deuteronomy built on the foundations of traditional Yahwism, but refined and rationalized it. Although its doctrine may not be that of formal monotheism — that is, the denial of the existence of any deity but one (though see Deut. 4:35, 39) — it constantly repeats its assertion that there is only one God for Israel. The exact meaning of 6:4, which is one of the most famous verses in the Old Testament and is daily recited by Jews in their prayers to this day, is much disputed. It is not clear whether the passage is saying that Yahweh alone is Israel's God or that Israel's God is, in an absolute sense, the only God. But the next verse, which is a command to Israel to devote itself without restraint to the love of Yahweh, is echoed incessantly throughout the book.

The fierce antagonism expressed in the book to the worship of other gods clearly presupposes that both in the past and up to the present polytheism had been widely practiced in Israel. There is ample evidence of this in the books of Kings and in some of the prophetic books. Ezek. 8, for example, records the practice of idolatrous rites in the temple of Jerusalem itself on the eve of its destruction in 587 B.C., and Isa. 57:3-8; 65:3-5 probably refer to the continuation of such practices even after the Exile. There is no agreement at present among scholars about the nature of Israel's religion (or religions) in preexilic times, although it is generally

91

recognized that Yahweh was not the only deity worshipped. Some maintain that Israelite religion in that period was essentially the same as Canaanite religion. Others point to the prevalence, though not the exclusive use, of proper names compounded with the name of Yahweh at that time, suggesting that although Yahweh may have been one among a number of other gods worshipped, he was probably recognized as the chief god. Some (e.g., Morton Smith, *Palestinian Parties and Politics;* Bernhard Lang, *Monotheism and the Prophetic Minority;* see also Mark S. Smith, *The Early History of God,* for a fuller account) postulate the existence of a "Yahweh-alone" movement led by prophets and others which originated as early as the time of Elijah in the ninth century, and which later became generally accepted. Deuteronomy was clearly a key factor in this development.

Equally abhorrent to the Deuteronomist are magical practices such as divination and necromancy (Deut. 18:10-14) and objects suggestive of pagan worship (16:21-22). But it is the former inhabitants of the land (e.g., 7:1-7, 16; 20:15-18) who are the principal objects of abhorrence. The people are commanded to destroy them, not leaving a single person alive. This is partly because it is to Israel and Israel alone that God has given the land, but mainly because it is these peoples who worship other gods and may persuade Israelites to do the same. This commandment is an extraordinary one. Von Rad saw it as part of an ancient tradition of "holy war" which is found in other texts. As such it would at least be understandable — if hardly attractive to the modern reader — in the context of a speech by Moses to Israel on the eve of the invasion of the land. But in the context of the book in its present form, it makes no sense if taken literally.

Whom could the Deuteronomist have meant in referring to these peoples, who had long ago faded from the scene in his day? Once it is granted that they stand for people of his own time who were polytheists or idolaters, it is not difficult to identify them — if not with precision — as non-Israelite elements of the community with whom it is forbidden to maintain friendly relations. In a postexilic situation in which Israel was no longer master of the land — though they still hoped to recover it — such foreign elements, dangerous to the true faith, were certainly present. The command to exterminate them, a reminiscence of a former tradition, is obviously rhetorical and theoretical. But it witnesses to the fierceness of the Deuteronomic conviction that the land is a gift from Yahweh to Israel alone, and that the true faith must be preserved and protected *at all costs* from contamination by foreign idolaters — for that faith is the condition for the fulfillment of the promises.

Despite this ruthlessness in the Deuteronomist's view of God, his understanding of God's inner nature is a refined one. For the Deuteronomist God is immanent, in that he is active in Israel's history, and far from remote. In Deut. 4:7, for example, Moses asks, "For what other great nation has a god so near to it as Yahweh our God is whenever we call to him?" Yet God is also transcendent. The Deuteronomist's view is identical with that of Deutero-Isaiah in insisting that Yahweh is essentially different from the gods of the other nations, which are "made by human hands, objects of wood and stone that neither see, nor hear, nor eat, nor smell" (Deut. 4:28; cf. 28:36, 64; 29:17). Yahweh is invisible. The people are told that when he addressed the people at Horeb, "You heard the sound of words but saw no form: there was only a voice" (4:12). This doctrine of the invisible God was probably not an original one. The principle that Yahweh should not be represented by an image seems to have been very ancient. But Deuteronomy makes the point with particular clarity.

Another aspect of Deuteronomy's doctrine of God's transcendence is supposedly what has been called its "name theology." This term refers especially to the manner in which God is present in the temple. In other religions of the ancient Near East a temple was literally the deity's house, in which he or she resided. In the Ugaritic epic of Baal, for example, Baal's desire to build a "house" for himself is a major theme. In the Old Testament too, the usual Hebrew term for the Jerusalem temple is *beth yhwh*, "Yahweh's house." It is also sometimes called his "palace" *(hekhal)*. As in the surrounding religions, it is the place where he "lives" *(yashabh)*. It is a striking fact that nowhere in Deuteronomy is this expression used of Yahweh's relationship to the temple, nor is the temple referred to as his house, except very occasionally in the laws — never in the specifically "theological" chs. 1-11. Rather, the Deuteronomist has his own way of describing it. For him, the one place in which Israel is to offer its public worship is regularly referred to simply as "the place that Yahweh your God will choose out of all your tribes to put his name there," or "to cause his name to dwell there" (12:5ff.). (Although it is not named in the book because the Mosaic fiction requires that it has not yet been chosen by Yahweh, it is probably to be assumed that the Jerusalem temple is meant.)

There has been much discussion of what is meant in Deuteronomy by the "name" of Yahweh (see T. N. D. Mettinger, *The Dethronement of Sabaoth*). The notion of a deity's name as somehow distinct from the deity in question yet still closely related to him or her is found in other ancient

Near Eastern religions, and in some cases the name comes close to being a separate deity itself. In the Old Testament it is frequently used simply as a synonym for God himself; and some scholars deny that the choice of this word in Deuteronomy has theological significance — that there is no "name theology" in this book.

Although the "name of Yahweh" which dwells on the earth in Yahweh's chosen place undoubtedly stands for the presence of Yahweh with his people, it is in heaven that he permanently resides. It was from heaven that he spoke to his people in the past to discipline them (4:36), and in ch. 26 the Israelite who has has brought the tithe of his produce to offer it "before Yahweh" (v. 13) prays: "Look down from your holy habitation, *from heaven,* and bless your people Israel and the ground that you have given us" (v. 15). It remains probable that the terminology used in Deuteronomy marks a movement away from a view that Yahweh, who is "God in heaven above and on the earth beneath" (4:39), might nevertheless be limited by a concept of holy space, while yet insisting strongly that he is active on earth in his bounty toward Israel.

Two central aspects of the doctrine of God in Deuteronomy are represented by the words "love" and "choose." Israel has been singled out from the nations of the world in that Yahweh has "set his love" upon Israel, and that he has chosen Israel to be his special people. These themes run through the whole book, and they are closely related. In 4:37 the people are told: "Because he loved your fathers and chose their children after them, he brought you out of Egypt by his great strength." But it is also made clear that this love and this selection of Israel are not due to any merit or greatness of theirs. It was not because Israel was a great and numerous people that God chose it. Indeed, since that choice was made Israel had not shown itself worthy of it, but had been continually rebellious.

Great emphasis is laid, especially in chs. 4ff., on what God has done, and on what he will do for his people in the future if they will now be obedient to his laws. No reason is given for God's choice of them. His love was antecedent and presumably needed no explanation. It is, however, traced back to the time of the patriarchs of Genesis — to the promise or oath that God had made to Abraham to give the land to his descendants (e.g., 1:8; 6:10; 9:5; 29:13; 30:20; 34:4). The first example of this love in action was the Exodus from Egypt, the first demonstration of what God could do for Israel. This choice of Israel was confirmed and reinforced by the encounter with him at Horeb, where they became his holy people and where the relationship was established and the covenant made, with its obligation to obedience to God's commands. God in turn then demonstrated his love and care for his people by leading them safely through the desert for forty years to the place where Moses was now addressing them, having dealt on the way with those nations that had opposed their progress.

But these historical retrospects do not constitute the central message of the book. They are essential to it in that they set out the character of the God who has chosen Israel and the proofs that he has already given them of his faithfulness despite their own unworthiness to receive these gifts. However, the emphasis of the book is not on the past but on the future. The chapter of Israel's past history is at an end, and they are asking what they may now expect from this God. The answer is that God will now extend his bounty to them and give them what has so long been promised: the possession of the land of Canaan. The richness and material abundance of that land are described in detail (8:7-9); and it is promised that "You shall eat your fill and bless Yahweh your God for the good land that he has given you" (v. 10). The book emphasizes that God has even prepared the land in advance for them. It contains cities, well-equipped houses, cisterns, vineyards, and olive groves built and planted by the Canaanites whom they are to dispossess. But the people are warned of the danger that in their enjoyment of these things they may forget what God has done for them (6:10-12).

Total obedience to God's commands from now on is essential to the people's well-being, and the commandments which occupy almost half the book are set out in great detail in the laws of chs. 12-26. This loving God can and will take back all that he has given them if they are disobedient — and much more than that. While 28:1-14 sets out the benefits that they will continue to enjoy if they are obedient, the much longer 28:15-68 describes the horrible fate that disobedience will bring on them. They will suffer crop failure and famine, pestilence and other diseases, despair, defeat and conquest by enemies, expulsion from the land and scattering among the nations, and even a return to Egypt and to renewed slavery there.

One of the most frequently used words in Deuteronomy is "today." It occurs almost a hundred times, most frequently in the phrase "the commandment that I am commanding you today." This usage is of great significance for the theological understanding of the book. Basically it is used to indicate the crucial nature of the moment at which the covenant at Horeb is established and the people are summoned to obedience. So in 11:26-28 Moses states, "See, I am setting before you *today* a blessing and a curse: the blessing, if you obey the commandments of Yahweh your God that I am commanding you today; and the curse, if you do not obey the commandments of Yahweh your God, but turn from the way that I am commanding you today." The people have a choice, and the consequences of the choice that they make are made clear to them. But the readers of the book in every subsequent generation are intended to understand the words as applying to themselves. When in 5:3 Moses affirms, "Not with our ancestors did Yahweh make this covenant, but with *us*, who are all of us here alive today," the contextual reference is to the preceding generations as compared with the present one. But the readers of the book would understand that the "with us" applied to them. They also are the heirs of the covenant with its obligations — the covenant is for all subsequent generations. There is an "actualization" here. The reader is to understand that that moment in the past and the present moment are one. To an exilic or postexilic readership this was, moreover, true of the whole book. They too were to live in hope of the (re-)possession of the land and the promises, the call to obedience, and the warnings about the consequences of disobedience applied to them as much as to their ancestors. In much the same way have both Jewish and Christian readers continued to believe.

The teaching of Deuteronomy about *Israel* and its relation to God has to some extent been dealt with already. It follows from Deuteronomy's understanding of the nature of God, and is expressed mainly in the use of two frequently recurring words: "choose" and "covenant."

The notion of choice, with its implication of freedom to determine one's own actions or mode of life, is one which is characteristic of Deuteronomy. God chooses, but human beings also have that freedom. Even a runaway slave may choose where he wishes to live (23:16). In 30:19, in one of the passages which set out the alternatives of obedience and disobedience and their respective consequences, the audience is urged (in an imperative in the singular, apparently addressed to the individual present in the crowd) to "choose life." But in the great majority of cases it is God who, in his sovereign freedom, exercises his choice. He chooses the place where he is to set his name; it is also God who chooses the kings to rule over the nation (17:15); and he chooses, or rather has chosen, Israel "out of all the peoples" to be a "holy people" and his "treasured possession" (7:6; 14:2).

The use of the verb "to choose" of Yahweh's relationship to the people as a whole in Deuteronomy is particularly significant. In the Deuteronomistic History (e.g., 1 Sam. 10:24; 16:8-10; 2 Sam. 6:21; 16:18) it is used of Yahweh's selection of Saul and of David. The verb is not so used of later Davidic kings, but the idea appears in Hos. 8:4 with regard to kings of northern Israel, and in the only passage that refers to kings in Deuteronomy (Deut. 17:14-20) it is used in the same way. But it is in Deuteronomy that the verb is first used of Yahweh's choice of the whole people of Israel, and used frequently and emphatically. This book — in common with some other late (exilic and postexilic) books such as Second Isaiah (Isa. 55:3-5) and Ezekiel, in whose blueprint of the future (Ezek. 40-48) there is only a "prince" with very limited functions — has, as it is often expressed, "democratized" the concept of divine choice. The ancient Near Eastern belief that divine choice and a special relationship with the gods was confined to kings, who as sacral figures were regarded as semi-divine and often as standing in a filial relationship to gods — a belief which has been to a large extent adopted with regard to the Davidic dynasty (cf. Ps. 2:7) — was now transferred to the whole nation, which had thus become a "holy people" (Deut. 7:6; 14:2, 21, etc.). Correspondingly, although Yahweh is not directly called Israel's father except in the poetical 32:6, in 1:31 and 8:5 he is likened to a father; and Israelites are commonly called "brothers" throughout the book.

The other term which is most frequently used to describe Israel's relationship with Yahweh is "covenant" (*berith*). In almost every case, the covenant referred to in Deuteronomy (e.g., 5:2) is that which had been made at Horeb (Sinai). In fact the entire book may be described as an exposition by Moses of the contents and meaning of that covenant. In ch. 29, however, there is reference to a *second* covenant now made, after the proclamation of the laws, in the land of Moab, a covenant made "*in addition to* the covenant that he had made with them at Horeb" (v. 1). The significance of, and the necessity for, this second covenant has never been satisfactorily explained. Deut. 29:9 commands the people to "diligently observe the words of this covenant, in order that you may succeed in everything that you do."

This second covenant is found nowhere else in the Old Testament. Various attempts at explaining it have been made, although the commentaries have tended to pass over the problem in silence; many scholars (e.g., Samuel R. Driver and von Rad) do, however, recognize the special character of this section of the book. It is widely held that ch. 29, perhaps together with ch. 30 or with other subsequent chapters as well, constitutes a kind of supplement or appendix to the laws. Klaus Baltzer (*The Covenant Formulary,* 34ff.) argued that chs. 29-30 are couched in the form of a treaty (see above), and they may in some sense have constituted an *alternative* to the postulate of the rest of the book, that it is the *Sinai* (Horeb) covenant which is in question. Others see the second covenant as simply a reinforcement or confirmation of the first. A. D. H. Mayes suggested that since new laws had been promulgated, a new covenant was needed to embrace them. Norbert Lohfink linked it to the appointment of Joshua as Moses' successor as noted in ch. 31; such an appointment would require a new covenant in which the promise of obedience was renewed. Whatever may be the solution of the problem, this second covenant detracts from the "once-and-for-all" character of the Horeb-Sinai covenant as presented in the rest of the book, and must be regarded as an unexplained anomaly.

Central to the theology of Deuteronomy is the theme of the *land*, which was promised to the ancestors and is now to be given to Israel for immediate occupation — though on condition of obedience to God's laws, and on the understanding that it will be taken away again in case of apostasy. As has been pointed out in chapter 4 above, this theme was of obvious relevance to a postexilic generation which had once possessed, but then lost, the land. Deuteronomy knows, and frequently alludes to, the promises to the patriarchs of Genesis. But its obsessive preoccupation with this theme and the atmosphere of expectancy produced by the imminence of the possession of the land exceed anything in Genesis. Only in this book is there a fully developed *theology* of the land, in which the entire future of the nation has now been concentrated.

The question of the antiquity of this tradition of the promise of the land is a disputed one. Claus Westermann, in a study of the promises in Genesis, argued that the promise of the land is among the latest developments of the theme and had its origin at a late period in the history of the religion of Israel. However that may be, it is only in Deuteronomy that the theme reached its fullest exposition. It is significant that only here is it closely tied to the promulgation of the laws. Deuteronomy is a book which is concerned with a particular present and a particular future. The laws are not given in a temporal vacuum; it is in the land which Israel is about to occupy that they are to be obeyed.

What Deuteronomy has to say about *worship* — or at least the way in which it expresses it — is revolutionary. The sacrificial cult for Deuteronomy is an expression of love for God and of gratitude for what he has done and is doing for his people. Other reasons for offering sacrifice that are found elsewhere in the Old Testament are passed over in silence here. It may seem strange that love for God in Deuteronomy is a duty — that the Israelites are commanded to love him (6:5). Some scholars have suggested that the word "love" here is a technical term taken over from the vassal treaties of the ancient Near East, where it means no more than to remain faithful to an overlord rather than to have loving feelings toward him; but this is hardly the case. In Deuteronomy the love is to be "with the heart and inner being (Hebrew *nephesh*) and strength" (6:5). Deuteronomy does not see this command to love God as a contradiction. It is in obeying God's command that one most truly expresses one's love for him.

Deuteronomy is concerned in its laws about worship with purity and singlemindedness. Earlier Israel had worshipped at a variety of places throughout the land, and there was no control over the purity of the worship offered there, even supposing that it had been offered solely to Yahweh. Now, in a world teeming with worship offered to other gods and with superstitious, magical practices, there must be a total ban on such behavior. All idolatrous worship must be rooted out and its practitioners destroyed (6:19; 7:5, 16, 22-25; 9:3; 12:2-3). This language can hardly, however, be other than symbolic; the readers of Deuteronomy were in any case in no position to carry out such destruction. But within Israel itself no idolatrous or magical practices were to be tolerated (4:16; 5:8; 16:21-22; 17:2-7; 18:10-14).

It was in order to secure purity of worship that public sacrificial worship was now to be restricted to one place (ch. 12). Whether or not attempts had been made earlier, by reforming kings such as Hezekiah and Josiah, to make Jerusalem the sole place of public worship, now it was absolutely commanded that it be offered only in "the place that Yahweh your God will choose to put his name there." Again, whether or not this was originally intended to refer to Jerusalem, it came to be so understood. In order to make this law a practicable one, a distinction was made between animals offered for sacrifice and animals slaughtered for food: the latter could be slaughtered at home and eaten, provided that the provision against eating the blood was observed (12:15-16). This also was an entirely new provision. Some have described it as a "secularization" of sacrifice, but this is a misunderstanding.

Deuteronomy more than any other Old Testament book concerns itself not only with the obligation to worship and the rules for doing so, but also with the subjective aspect of worship — with the feelings of the worshipper and the spirit in which he or she worships. There is often a personal note in those passages that deal with public worship. It is regularly stated that these are occasions for rejoicing (e.g., 12:7, 12, 18; 14:26;

16:11, 14; 26:11; 27:7). The rejoicing is closely connected with another feeling, that of gratitude to God.

But there are also times for the *individual* to draw near to God in prayerful reflection, not necessarily associated with public worship. An individual in distress is assured that even when he has seriously transgressed he can find God in his heart: "You will find him if you search after him with all your heart and soul" (4:29). In other passages the *nearness* of the worshipper to God is emphasized: "For what other great nation has a god so near to it as Yahweh our God is whenever we call to him?" (4:7; cf. 30:11-14). There is nothing automatic or impersonal in the worship of God as described in Deuteronomy.

Both instruction in the laws and participation in worship were matters for *family* activity in Deuteronomy. In 6:6-9 the people are to teach the laws to their children in the context of family life — at home, when away from home, when getting up in the morning, and when going to bed. In 6:20-25 the child who asks about the meaning of the laws is to be told how God saved Israel from slavery in Egypt and then gave them the laws for their own well-being. This personal and family note is found also in ch. 12, in the law about worship: the whole family shares in the rejoicing and the feasting at the place designated by God for worship.

Further treatment of the laws of Deuteronomy will be found in chapter 7 below. Here they will be considered in their theological aspect — that is, as they directly reflect Deuteronomy's main theological concerns. These may be summarized in the phrase "one God, one people, one land, one place of worship." This insistence on oneness has been called "centralization"; a better description might be "unification." At the same time, there is a concern for the individual in Deuteronomy's theology, and this finds expression also in the laws. (It should be remarked at this point that many of these provisions were not entirely new, although they often appear here in a more highly developed form than in earlier legislation.)

As it gives practical expression to the oneness of the deity in its laws concerning worship, so Deuteronomy gives practical expression to the oneness of the people in prescribing a unified political and social order. It lays down rules for the judiciary and the administration of justice and for the selection, qualifications, and functions of the leading figures in the united community: king, judges, priests and Levites, and prophets. As has already been pointed out, the book also makes certain regulations for the family.

The law of the king is contained in 17:14-20. It is of interest to note that there is no reference to a king of Israel anywhere else in the Pentateuch. Evidently the author of this passage took it for granted that, like other nations (v. 14), Israel would again have a monarchy; but this monarchy would reflect the theological principles of the book. Future kings would have none of either the sacral qualities or the political powers which earlier kings had claimed for themselves. Indeed, nothing at all is said about either political or military authority. These kings must be approved or "chosen" by God (v. 15). As members of the community ("brothers"), they must not claim superior status (v. 20) and must not emulate their predecessors in wealth and grandeur or in the possession of numerous wives (vv. 16-17). They are to possess a written copy of "this law" and study it regularly with the help of the Levites. Above all, they must scrupulously obey all the laws in this book (vv. 19-20). In other words, the ultimate authority in Israel is the law, not the king, who may be presumed to be no more than a kind of superior civil servant.

Deuteronomy is passionately concerned about *justice* (Hebrew *tsedeq, mishpat*): "Justice, and only justice, you shall pursue" (16:20, which makes this a condition of living and prospering in the land). This follows from the doctrine of Israel as a community of "brothers" equal before God. In 16:18-20 the administration of justice is put on a systematic basis by the command to appoint judges and "officials" "throughout your tribes, in all your towns" who will be impartial and incorruptible, so that no one shall be deprived from seeking justice in the courts. (A similar action is claimed in 2 Chr. 19:5-7 as an innovation by King Jehoshaphat of Judah.)

But it is not only in the law courts that individual rights are to be protected, nor does the law stop at legal rights. Love is also required. In particular, both protection and material help are to be given to individuals who most need it: orphans, widows, strangers, slaves, poor laborers, and the poor in general (Deut. 15:4-11). Deut. 15:4 even seems to assert that owing to such generosity poverty will cease to exist: "There will be no poor among you," although v. 11 must recognize that this is an unattainable ideal.

These laws (some of which are not peculiar to Deuteronomy) have been described as "humanitarian"; but this modern term is not entirely appropriate. It is rather a question of gratitude. The Israelites are to put themselves in the place of the unfortunate and remember how they as a people were once in a similar helpless plight: "Remember that you were a slave in Egypt and Yahweh your God redeemed you from there; therefore I command you to do this" (24:18); "You shall love the stranger, for you were strangers in the land of Egypt" (10:19). The implication is that the memory of God's love for Israel in the past should color the Israelite's life in the present and the future.

Deuteronomy's view of the *priesthood* is not totally revolutionary. Most of its functions are identical with those prescribed in Exodus-Numbers; but the emphasis has significantly shifted. It is notable that Deuteronomy devotes little space to the details of sacrificial worship compared with Exodus-Numbers, although it may be presumed that the priests continued to preside over it in a similar way. There also seems to have been a widening of the membership of the priestly class, since several texts appear to identify the priests with the Levites, who in the legislation of Exodus-Numbers occupy an inferior position.

In Deuteronomy the non-sacrificial functions of the priesthood are greatly emphasized, and in fact the priests have become the supreme civil authority. They are associated with the civil judges in 17:8-13 and 19:17 in giving decisions on difficult cases and in serious cases such as that of murder. However, they appear to outrank the judges, since they are mentioned first when the two functionaries are named together. In 17:12 it is the priests alone who are mentioned as imposing the death penalty, and in 21:5 cases of dispute and assault are dealt with by them alone. It is they who instruct the people about the law. They are concerned in providing a copy of the law for the newly appointed king, who seems to be under their direction (17:18). It is they who assemble the people for the public reading of the law every seven years (31:10-13). The priests address the people before battle with the assurance that God will fight for them (20:2-4). They bless the people (21:5; 27:12), but also proclaim a series of curses against those who transgress (27:13).

Prophets, as has been noted above, are mentioned in Deuteronomy only in two extended passages (13:1-5; 18:15-22), and also in a single verse (34:10). In 34:10 Moses himself is said to be a prophet, the greatest who has yet arisen in Israel (cf. also 18:15, 18). There is no evidence that Deuteronomy envisages the establishment of an actual prophetic institution. The statement by Moses in 18:15 that God "will raise up for you a prophet like me" probably refers to the future appearance of prophets from time to time rather than to the expectation of a single, particular prophet.

Clearly prophecy was a current phenomenon at the time when these passages were written, but it is difficult to say what were the particular historical circumstances that lay behind these particular laws. Von Rad in his commentary could offer no answer to this question; he remarked that

"It is not easy to say what kind of prophets the preacher in Deuteronomy has in mind" (*Deuteronomy*, 97). Both passages have affinities with utterances of Jeremiah, who had to struggle against the false prophets of his time, in the last days of the monarchy before its fall in 587. These false prophets included those who, in opposition to Jeremiah, attempted to buoy up the confidence of their audience with promises that the Babylonians would not capture Jerusalem, and those who frankly prophesied in the name of other gods than Yahweh (Jer. 14:13-16; 23:9-17; 27:9-18; 28:8-9). In Deuteronomy the warnings against prophets who told lies and who tried to persuade their audience to turn to the worship of other gods are no less vehement; but the polemic is more generalized, and directed more toward an undefined future than to an actual situation. It is, however, interesting that in both books the crucial question is raised — and hardly satisfactorily answered — how false prophets may be identified and distinguished from true prophets.

The functions of the true prophet in Deuteronomy are to act as a spokesman of Yahweh, who has "put his words in his mouth," and to predict the future. But in this book the words of God are primarily the words of the law; the aim of the false prophet is to turn his hearers away from "the way in which Yahweh your God commanded you to walk" (Deut. 13:5). It is Moses, the spokesman of the law, who is the greatest of the prophets (34:10). So prophecy is not, as in the prophetic books of the Old Testament, to be so much an ad hoc message from God but a proclamation of the law, which is the supreme religious authority.

A significant innovation of Deuteronomy is that its laws are to be written in a book (28:58, 61; 30:10; 31:24), which is to be kept beside the ark "as a witness against you" (31:26) and to be read publicly at seven-year intervals (31:9-11) in an assembly of the whole people. The only other reference in the Pentateuch to such a "book" is in Exod. 24, where it is stated that Moses "wrote down all the words of Yahweh" and then, in the context of a covenant-making ceremony, "took the book of the covenant, and read it in the hearing of the people," who solemnly promised to obey its laws (Exod. 24:7-8). Some scholars, including von Rad, saw here an ancient, premonarchical, tradition; but others (e.g., Nicholson, *Deuteronomy and Tradition*, 70-72) consider this passage to be an addition to the book inserted by one who followed the tradition of Deuteronomy.

As has been already noted, Deuteronomy contains the most comprehensive body of laws in the Pentateuch. It is clearly intended to be consulted for guidance on many aspects of daily life, in sharp contrast with the laws of Leviticus, which are very restricted in scope and mainly concern the functions of the priesthood. Also, whether the seven-year public reading ever took place or not, Deuteronomy makes the laws available to the whole people. It marks the beginning of that devotion to the Torah as the authoritative word of God which has remained a feature of Judaism to this day, and has also been a formative influence on Christian views about the authority of Scripture.

The *style* and *language* of Deuteronomy are extremely distinctive, though they are also characteristic of the so-called Deuteronomistic literature, especially the Deuteronomistic History, and also parts of some of the prophetic books. So distinctive are they that they are immediately recognizable even to readers who know no Hebrew. Here are some of the most distinctive phrases: "that your days may be long . . . "; "which I am commanding you today"; "so you shall purge the evil from your midst"; "the place which Yahweh your God will choose"; "do what is right/evil in the sight of Yahweh"; "the priests and the Levites"; "with all your heart and with all your soul"; "the land that you are entering to occupy" (see the more complete list in S. R. Driver, *Introduction to the Literature of the Old Testament*). Another distinctive feature of the book is of course the homiletic or preaching style, especially in the first eleven chapters; there is a sense in which the whole book is a sermon placed in the mouth of Moses.

For Further Reading

Baltzer, Klaus. *The Covenant Formulary in Old Testament, Jewish, and Early Christian Writings*. Philadelphia: Fortress and Oxford: Blackwell, 1971. (First published in German, 1964.)

Blenkinsopp, Joseph. *The Pentateuch: An Introduction to the First Five Books of the Bible*. New York: Doubleday and London: SCM, 1992, ch. 6.

Clements, Ronald E. *Deuteronomy*. OTG. Sheffield: JSOT Press, 1989.

Driver, Samuel R. *A Critical and Exegetical Commentary on Deuteronomy*. 2nd ed. ICC. Edinburgh: T. & T. Clark and New York: Scribner's, 1902.

———. *Introduction to the Literature of the Old Testament*. 8th ed. Edinburgh: T. & T. Clark, 1909.

Lang, Bernhard. *Monotheism and the Prophetic Minority*. Sheffield: Almond, 1983.

McCarthy, Dennis J. *Old Testament Covenant: A Survey of Current Opinions.* Richmond: John Knox and Oxford: Blackwell, 1972.

————. *Treaty and Covenant.* Analecta Biblica 21. Rome: Pontifical Biblical Institute Press, 1963. Rev. ed., 1978.

Mayes, A. D. H. *Deuteronomy.* NCBC. London: Marshall, Morgan & Scott, 1979, and Grand Rapids: Wm. B. Eerdmans, 1981.

Mendenhall, George E. "Covenant Forms in Israelite Tradition," *BA* 17 (1954): 50-76. Repr. in *The BA Reader* 3, ed. E. F. Campbell, Jr., and David Noel Freedman. Garden City: Doubleday, 1970, 25-53.

Mettinger, T. N. D. *The Dethronement of Sabaoth.* Coniectanea Biblica, Old Testament 18. Lund: Gleerup, 1982.

Nicholson, Ernest W. *Deuteronomy and Tradition.* Philadelphia: Fortress and Oxford: Blackwell, 1967.

————. *Exodus and Sinai in History and Tradition.* Richmond: John Knox and Oxford: Blackwell, 1973.

Noth, Martin. *The Deuteronomistic History.* JSOT Supplement 15. Sheffield: JSOT Press, 1981. (Translated from the 2nd German ed., 1957.)

von Rad, Gerhard. *Deuteronomy.* OTL. Philadelphia: Westminster and London: SCM, 1966. (First published in German, 1964.)

————. "The Form-Critical Problem of the Hexateuch," in *The Problem of the Hexateuch and Other Essays.* Edinburgh: Oliver & Boyd, 1966, 1-78. Repr. Philadelphia: Fortress and London: SCM, 1984. (First published in German, 1938.)

————. *Studies in Deuteronomy.* SBT, 1st series 9. Chicago: Regnery and London: SCM, 1953. (First published in German, 1948.)

Rendtorff, Rolf. *The Old Testament: An Introduction.* London: SCM, 1985, and Philadelphia: Fortress, 1986. (First published in German, 1983.)

Smith, George Adam. *The Book of Deuteronomy.* CBSC. Cambridge: Cambridge University Press, 1918.

Smith, Mark S. *The Early History of God: Yahweh and the Other Deities in Ancient Israel.* San Francisco: Harper & Row, 1990.

Smith, Morton. *Palestinian Parties and Politics That Shaped the Old Testament.* New York: Columbia University Press, 1971. 2nd ed., London: SCM, 1987.

Weinfeld, Moshe. *Deuteronomy and the Deuteronomic School.* Oxford: Clarendon Press, 1972. Repr. Winona Lake: Eisenbrauns, 1992.

Welch, Adam C. *The Code of Deuteronomy.* London: Oxford University Press, 1924.

————. *Deuteronomy: The Framework to the Code.* London: Milford, 1932.

Westermann, Claus. *The Promises to the Fathers.* Philadelphia: Fortress, 1980. (First published in German, 1976.)

CHAPTER 7

The Laws

Aᴌᴌ ᴛʜᴇ ʟᴀᴡꜱ in the Pentateuch have been inserted into narrative contexts to which they did not originally belong. (The laws of Deuteronomy only appear to be an exception. Although it is true that in this case the laws came first and the book later, the fact remains that they are presented in the context of the wider account of Moses' life.) They belong, in fact, to a quite distinct genre, one which is found in abundance in the ancient Near Eastern documents that have come down to us.

Martin Noth in his work on the laws of the Pentateuch was well aware that when used of the ancient Near Eastern world the term "law" is a somewhat misleading one. (He regularly put the word in quotation marks to indicate this fact.) None of the several "law codes" in question (see translations in *ANET,* 159-198, and its Supplement, 523-26) is, or was intended to be, a "statute book" on the basis of which the king or the judges appointed by him were required to make their decisions in the law courts. In view of the similarities between the laws of the Pentateuch and these other collections of laws, it is necessary to discuss briefly the nature and purpose of the ancient Near Eastern laws before considering how far the Old Testament laws corresponded to or differed from them in this respect.

These "law codes" — Sumerian, Babylonian, Assyrian, and Hittite — cover a long period, ranging from the late third millennium B.C. to the Neo-Babylonian period, which ended in the late sixth century. They thus attest to a single common, long-standing legal tradition in the ancient Near East which developed gradually over the centuries. Unfortunately there is no consensus of opinion about the purposes of these codes. It has been suggested that they were intended as a kind of royal apologia, praising particular kings for their concern for justice. But not all of them have been found — as was the Code of Hammurabi — on public monuments, where they might have been inscribed for perusal by a (literate) public. Others have been found on small cuneiform clay tablets, in a form more suitable for deposit in archives or libraries, and have no prologue or epilogue explaining their purpose.

Another theory is that the codes were based on actual legal judgments and were thus available to judges for consultation in difficult cases. Yet very few of the extant legal documents, which are very numerous, ever refer specifically to the codes. A third view is that the codes are purely literary documents created by learned scribes, composed out of a love of systematization and classification in general, and not intended for practical use. According to some scholars, this may be suggested by the way in which the texts sometimes indulge in elaborations of what appear to be no more than hypothetical cases. In fact, legal judgments were probably made on an oral basis, though decisions were often recorded in writing.

Whatever may have been the reason for these legal compilations (and they may not all have been compiled for the same purpose), there can be no doubt that they refer — whether in reality or hypothetically — to the laws of the state, that is, of the king, who was the supreme political authority and the chief judge, responsible for law and order. Although (e.g., in the Code of Hammurabi) the king may be represented as receiving the laws from a god, in practical terms the king was the lawgiver.

It is a remarkable fact that nowhere in the Old Testament is the king represented as having anything to do with the making of laws. Kings were the chief judges as elsewhere, and are pictured as making oral decisions, though not specifically with reference to written laws (e.g., 2 Sam. 14:1-11; 15:3-5; 1 Kgs. 3:16-28). Also, according to 2 Chr. 19:8-11 Jehoshaphat of Judah appointed judges, drawn from the priests, Levites, and heads of families, to give judgment on disputed cases which the local courts had been unable to solve. But according to the Deuteronomistic History, the kings were themselves in no way above the law but subject to it and judged by it, and were frequently condemned by prophets for breaches of it. In Deut. 17:19 it is explicitly stated that the king has to obey the (Mosaic) law. Admittedly, one cannot be certain that the Deuteronomistic literature has correctly represented the state of affairs during the monarchy; and specific references to "the law" as the standard by which kings are judged occur not in the narrative sections of the Deuteronomistic History but in the editors' comments on and assessments of the reigns of particular kings.

Nevertheless, it is unlikely that the Deuteronomistic historians should have so altered their narrative sources as to have expunged any references to royal legislation which might originally have stood there.

A unique characteristic of the Pentateuchal laws is that they are represented as having been communicated to the whole people directly by God in connection with the making of the covenant — mostly through the mediation of Moses, who simply repeated to the people the words which God had spoken to him, but in some cases with no mediation at all. In a few cases in Leviticus and Numbers laws are addressed to Moses, to Moses and Aaron, or to the priests. However, their administration was necessarily in the hands of particular leaders whose identity varied from time to time with changes in the political conditions under which the nation lived. Many of the laws prescribe specific penalties for persons who breached them, including the death penalty.

Lawmaking in Israel undoubtedly had a long history. Some laws may have originated before a national state existed, as rules governing certain aspects of behavior in a tribal society that were or were not allowable in the interests of community solidarity. It has been suggested (e.g., by Erhard S. Gerstenberger) that some types of Israelite law share a common origin with early wisdom, especially those laws prohibiting such things as theft, murder, and sexual transgressions which would disrupt tribal and family harmony. Such rules would have been made under the authority of heads of clans and families.

Later there developed a system of local officials who had authority to decide cases and, when necessary, to exact penalties for breach of the laws. Deuteronomy speaks of priests, judges, and officials in this connection; the complex system of laws about such things as sacrifice and purity would naturally be in the charge of the priests. During the monarchy and even later, the main judicial authorities appear to have been the elders or heads of families who administered justice in the town gate; appeals to a higher court seem to have been quite exceptional. In Deuteronomy the elders deal with such cases as those of a stubborn and rebellious son (Deut. 21:18-21), and of a wife accused of not having been a virgin before marriage (22:13-21), both of which carried the penalty of death by stoning. They also decided "civil" cases such as the refusal of a man to marry his deceased brother's widow (25:5-10), and also of unsolved murders (21:1-6). The institution of the elders as judges apparently served to remove such jurisdiction from the sole hands of the head of a family, making it a community matter. This continued in a somewhat different form until very late times, as is shown by such incidents in the New Testament as the stoning of Stephen for blasphemy (Acts 7:54-60), and of the woman taken in adultery (John 8:1-11), where elements of the population could incite both elders and people to put supposed offenders to death by stoning.

The judicial system in operation during the postexilic period is not clearly understood; but clearly there will have been major changes under Persian rule in Judah and with the breakdown of the whole political system that had prevailed before the destruction. We are told that Ezra, who was both a priest and "a scribe skilled in the law of Moses that Yahweh the God of Israel had given" (Ezra 7:6), was sent to Jerusalem by the Persian king Artaxerxes to "make inquiries about Judah and Jerusalem according to the law of your God" (v. 14), and that he was given authority to appoint magistrates and judges with the power to execute those who refused to obey "the law of your God and the law of the king" (vv. 25-26). We are told also that Nehemiah, another emissary sent from Artaxerxes and who is referred to as "governor," was also assiduous in seeing that the law was enforced.

Apart from these scraps of information little is known about the administration of the law during the rest of the postexilic period. But it is clear that during this time the attitude toward the law of Moses underwent considerable change. Eventually, although many of its provisions were now out of date and no longer literally applicable to the new conditions of life, the law came to be regarded as a timeless entity which stood at the center of the new Judaism and which was binding, in as far as it could be observed, on all Jews. But this obedience had now become an individual obligation rather than a communal one.

Two Types of Law

One of the most important contributions to the understanding of the nature and history of the legal portions of the Pentateuch was the observation made by Albrecht Alt (1940) of the existence of two quite distinct types of law that are found together in these collections. The distinction between the two types, which he called "casuistic" and "apodictic," is a formal one; but Alt argued that the difference in form points to a difference of origin and of (original) purpose. Later scholars have disputed some aspects of Alt's formal classification, and the details of this discussion cannot be dealt with in this short survey; but there is still a general agreement about the existence of these two main types. The clearest and most frequent examples of the two are those which begin with the words "If a man . . ." (casuistic) and those which begin "You shall (not) . . ." (apodictic).

The simplest kind of casuistic law in the Pentateuch begins by stating a hypothetical — but entirely conceivable — specific case requiring a legal decision and then goes on to prescribe the appropriate verdict. For example:

> If (or "when") a slaveowner strikes the eye of a male or female slave, destroying it, the owner shall let the slave go, a free person, to compensate for the eye. (Exod. 21:26)
>
> If a man is caught lying with the wife of another man, both of them shall die (i.e., receive capital punishment). (Deut. 22:22)

There are variations in the form in which the laws are expressed (e.g., some laws which are probably to be classed as casuistic begin with a participle instead of with a conditional clause). Further, in some cases (e.g., Exod. 21:22-25; Deut. 22:23-27) a casuistic law is extended to cover particular or extenuating circumstances in which the action is deemed to have taken place and to vary the penalty accordingly. The similarities in form and often of matters dealt with, though not usually of penalties prescribed, between the casuistic laws of the Pentateuch and those of other ancient Near Eastern, especially Mesopotamian, casuistic laws (e.g., the Code of Hammurabi) leave no doubt that they belong to the same legal tradition. This type of law is not unique to Israel. But equally, it is improbable that direct borrowing from so far afield has taken place.

This legal tradition, stretching back to the third millennium, is of course much older than any of the Pentateuchal laws; and it has been suggested that Israelite casuistic law is in fact a Canaanite legacy. This may at first seem highly improbable, since no law codes have been found in any of the extant written material (mainly from Ras Shamra-Ugarit) from that region. Indeed, no evidence has come to light which indicates that law codes existed in Palestine or its environs before the appearance of Israelite laws. Nevertheless, the theory of a Canaanite source is plausible. The lack of relevant finds may be simply due to the chanciness of archaeological investigation, and Canaanite law codes may yet be discovered. Canaan would be a much more probable source of an Israelite casuistic law governing daily life than distant Assyria or Babylonia; and it is widely agreed that the Canaanite cities of the pre-Israelite period, with their high culture and position in the Semitic world, should not have lacked a legal system comparable with that of the surrounding peoples.

This "Canaanite" theory remains a strong possibility, whatever may be the truth about the origins of the Israelite people — whether they entered the land from outside or whether they were indigenous, having once belonged to the civilized life of the Canaanite city-states but having for some reason detached themselves from it. There can be no doubt that the culture of the Canaanite city-states which eventually became incorporated into the Israelite state profoundly influenced Israel, and that there were remarkable continuities in more than one cultural, as well as religious, field. Such borrowing of case law would also account for the existence of the two types of law postulated by Alt. The origin of the case law would be quite different from that of apodictic law, which may be seen as having developed from Israel's own unique tribal traditions.

The origins of these apodictic laws, however, are more obscure than those of the casuistic ones. There has been much debate also about the correctness of Alt's classification. The main characteristic of the apodictic laws is that they are categorical, not dealing with specific hypothetical cases but making an absolute demand. But, although he distinguished them totally from the casuistic laws, Alt admitted that they are quite varied in form. He divided them formally into four types.

1. The participial form mentioned above, for example:

Whoever strikes [participle] father or mother shall be put to death. (Exod. 21:15)

This type is now — partly because it prescribes the penalty — considered by many scholars to be a casuistic type, or perhaps a mixture of the two categories.

2. A second form is the curse. A prime example is Deut. 27:15-26, a series beginning:

Cursed be anyone who dishonors (participle) father or mother.

Here the penalty is not prescribed specifically, but is implied; however, the death sentence is presumed to be carried out not by human hands but directly by God himself.

3. A third major category is that which begins with, or contains, the words "You shall . . .," for example:

You shall not permit a female sorcerer to live. (Exod. 22:18)
You shall not revile God, or curse a leader of your people. (Exod. 22:28)
Three times in the year you shall hold a festival for me. (Exod. 23:14)

4. Alt placed the Decalogue or Ten Commandments (Exod. 20:3-17; Deut. 5:7-21) in a separate category.

It is now recognized that these different types of formation cannot simply be classed as belonging to a single, "apodictic" category. Any discussion of original purpose and function must take these differences into account. Recent study of extant Near Eastern documents has shown the need for modification of Alt's view that there are no parallels at all between the apodictic laws of the Pentateuch and these texts. For example, some Near Eastern vassal treaties contain stipulations which correspond in effect either to the Pentateuchal curses or to the prohibitions, although their form does not exactly correspond (see, e.g., George E. Mendenhall, H.-J. Boecker, Dennis J. McCarthy).

Alt held that the origin of the apodictic laws is a cultic one. This view is supported, at least to some extent, by the fact that the series of curses in Deut. 27:15-26 is represented as taking the form of a cultic ceremony in which the people respond to each curse with "Amen." This ceremony, however, is not actually part of the events of Sinai, to which all the laws have become attached in the process of the composition of the book. Rather, it is part of Moses' prescriptions for the *future*. The people are to perform it, on entering the land, at a prescribed place: standing on the two mountains of Ebal and Gerizim in the vicinity of Shechem. The most natural explanation of this scenario is that it goes back to a ritual action actually performed at some time at that place. By contrast, the series of laws at Lev. 18:6-23 prohibiting particular sexual irregularities in the family suggests a quite different origin. It may represent a code of rules which originally had their setting within a limited family or clan circle, possibly promulgated by the head of the family. Then again, it may be an example of freely agreed self-government by a small group, setting limits to what was acceptable behavior and so intended to maintain cohesion and harmony within that group. Yet again, the "participial" laws prescribing the death penalty suggest the more properly legal situation of a larger group in which such extreme sanctions were inevitable. In this respect the participial laws do at least bear a resemblance to the casuistic laws.

The question of the original setting and purpose of these so-called apodictic laws continues to be a subject of scholarly discussion. Their origins are probably quite diverse, and the lack of positive evidence makes it unlikely that agreement will be reached. One feature, however, is quite evident. In many cases groups of laws, sometimes in groups of ten or twelve, stand out prominently from their contexts as self-contained entities — a sign, if one were needed, that these collections of laws are the result of a complex and probably gradual compilation and development.

Whatever may have been the origins of the various laws and collections of laws in the Pentateuch, the significant fact is that they have all been brought into relationship with the making of the covenant at Sinai-Horeb and the person of Moses. Only in one place in the Old Testament is there a collection of laws which has no connection with the Mosaic covenant: Ezek. 40-48. It is this association with Moses and the making of the covenant at the beginning of Israel's history that makes the Torah the foundation document of the Bible. The foundations of the traditional faith of the Jews were laid down once and for all at Sinai, and there is a sense in which everything that happened subsequently was secondary. The later history of Israel was seen wholly in terms of obedience and disobedience to the Law, which was the complete revelation of God's will for his people. Although new circumstances eventually necessitated the creation of a massive literature of interpretation of the Law and of adaptation to it, this was commentary: nothing essential could be added to it or taken away from it (Deut. 4:2; 12:32). After the loss of the First Temple and of the monarchy in the sixth century B.C., and still more after the destruction of the Second Temple in A.D. 70, the Law became the one stable factor and the central pillar of Jewish life.

But the context in which the laws have been set is not simply that of God's demands on his people. It is also that of God's past gifts to his people, which certainly put Israel under an obligation to present and future obedience, but which are also a token both of God's power and of his willingness to continue to shower benefits on them. In particular, in all these collections of laws there are references to God's deliverance of Israel from slavery in Egypt, so that even laws which may have originally had no specifically Israelite character now bear the marks of the Yahwistic faith. In all kinds of contexts the people are to remember their deliverance from Egypt, and to frame their present and future conduct in the light of that event.

This connection with the deliverance from Egypt is explicitly made with regard to the whole body of commandments, for example, in Lev. 18:3; Num. 14:41; and most notably in the opening chapters of Deuteronomy. It is also made in the preface to the Decalogue in both of its versions: "I am Yahweh your God, who brought you out of the land of Egypt, out of the house of slavery; you shall have no other gods before me . . ." (Exod. 20:2-3; Deut. 5:6-7). (In Deut. 1-11 it is not only the Exodus that is cited, but also God's guidance of the people in their journey through the wilderness.) But the Exodus paradigm is also attached to various particular laws. Thus Lev. 11:45, in a chapter dealing with clean and unclean animals, relates the Exodus to the requirement to be holy as God himself is holy. Most frequently the connection is made with regard to laws requiring humane treatment of the poor and oppressed, whether Israelite or foreign residents in Israel; the people are reminded that they themselves had been poor, oppressed, aliens, and slaves in Egypt until Yahweh rescued them (Exod. 23:9; Lev. 19:33-34; 25:39-46; Deut. 15:12-15; 24:17-18). The Feast of Unleavened Bread is to be observed in the month Abib, reminding the people that it was in that month that they came out of Egypt. There are also reminders of the Exodus in connection with honest trading, a requirement that was not in itself a peculiarly Israelite requirement (Lev. 19:35-37), but also with the food laws, which were (Lev. 11:44-45). It is clear that the admonition to remember God's past acts of redemption applied to the whole life of Israel — to righteousness and morality as well as to private thoughts, public worship, and the education of children.

The Decalogue

The Decalogue, or the Ten Commandments as this short collection of laws is popularly known, occupies a special place among the Pentateuchal laws, as is apparent from the fact that it occurs twice: in Exod. 20:2-17 and Deut. 5:6-21. It has given rise in modern times to an immense quantity of scholarly literature.

The differences between the two versions are small. The main difference is in the reason given for the Fourth Commandment, on the observance of the sabbath. According to Exodus, this is to be a commemoration of God's rest on the seventh day after his works of creation (Exod. 20:11; cf. Gen. 2:2-3). However, in Deuteronomy it is — once again — the memory of slavery in Egypt that is invoked, presumably mainly as a reason for giving freedom to the individual's family, dependents, and domestic animals to have a regular break from work (Deut. 5:14-15). Otherwise the two versions are practically identical, although there are a few minor differences: the Fifth Commandment is slightly longer in Deuteronomy (5:16) than in Exodus (20:12), and in the Tenth Commandment Deuteronomy (5:21) but not Exodus (20:17) puts the wife before the house in the law forbidding the coveting of a neighbor's possessions.

The arrangement of laws in groups of ten or approximately ten (perhaps twelve may also have been deemed an appropriate number) is not entirely unusual in the Pentateuch. It is not this that makes this Decalogue distinctive. Such groupings were especially characteristic of apodictic prohibitions of the "You shall not . . ." kind. Such may be the group of laws regulating sexual relations in Lev. 18:7-18. Another series is to be found in Exod. 34:14-26, sometimes referred to as the "Ritual Decalogue" in distinction from the "Ethical Decalogue"; it is called "the ten commandments" in v. 28 and was inscribed by Moses at God's dictation on the second set of tablets that replaced the broken ones. The collection in Exod. 34 has some laws in common with the "Ethical Decalogue," but focuses more on cultic matters. The Decalogue in Exod. 20 and Deut. 5 consists mainly of prohibitions, but not entirely so; the Fourth and Fifth Commandments, on the sabbath and on honoring parents, are *positive* laws. The suggestion that originally these also were expressed in negative terms has nothing to commend it.

Much more, however, is to be said for the view that the Decalogue as it stands in Exod. 20 and Deut. 5 is an expansion of an earlier form, and many attempts have been made to reconstitute the text of that earlier form (e.g., M. E. Andrew, Eduard Nielsen). It is significant that five of the laws (in Exod. 20, vv. 3, 13-16) consist each of a single sentence containing a brief general command or prohibition. The other five (vv. 4, 7, 8-12, 17) have additional clauses that elaborate the prohibition with further detail, add emphasis to it, or give a reason for it. These may originally have read as follows:

You shall not make for yourself an idol.
You shall not make wrongful use of Yahweh's name.
Remember the sabbath day, and keep it holy.
Honor your father and your mother.
You shall not covet.

116

In Exod. 20 the Decalogue has been placed at the most crucial point in the Sinai story: the making of the covenant itself. It is represented not as commandments given to Moses and subsequently relayed by him to the people, but as spoken by God directly to the people in the midst of the thunder and lightning and sound of the trumpet emanating from the smoking mountain (Exod. 20:18-19). In Deut. 5 it forms part of a speech to the people by Moses in the plains of Moab, in which he reminds them of what God had said to them at Horeb. Not all modern scholars, however, believe that the Exodus Decalogue is the older of the two. Apart from the question whether the Decalogue in its present forms is derived from an older original, there is evidence that the present texts may have influenced one another in the course of transmission. Deuteronomic influence has been detected in both.

It is not at all clear what was the original setting of the Decalogue, its original purpose, or when it was composed. While some scholars (e.g., H. H. Rowley, Anthony Phillips) associate it with Moses himself, others see it as a late composition, assembled as a compendium of general behavior formed by excerpts from other laws in the Pentateuch. It has also been suggested that the Decalogue's original content was of a general nature, and that more specific laws such as that concerning sabbath observance were added later. It is, for example, observable that several of the laws are not specifically associated with Yahweh, and that others also may not have had a specific connection with him in their supposedly original shorter form. This may suggest that Gerstenberger is correct in supposing that the Decalogue — or part of it — had its origin in family or clan rules governing what was, or was not, acceptable behavior in such circles. In its present form, however, it is significant that the list is headed by the laws which forbid the worship of other gods or their images.

One theory, that of Phillips, that the Decalogue "constituted ancient Israel's preexilic criminal law code given to her at Sinai" (*Ancient Israel's Criminal Law*, 1) must be judged improbable. Instead, the Decalogue falls in the category, already discussed, of apodictic "laws" which are not laws in the usual sense of the word. No penalties are prescribed as with the casuistic and some other laws of the Pentateuch, or with such other laws as could be applied in a court of law. Also, some of the laws are imprecise (e.g., "Honor your father and your mother") or appear to refer not to indictable offenses but simply to thoughts and desires (e.g., "You shall not covet"; the view of J. J. Stamm that this verb has here roughly the same meaning as "steal" is improbable, if only because this would cause a duplication with the Eighth Commandment). Again, murder, adultery, theft, and false witness are actions forbidden in most cultures (see also ancient Near Eastern wisdom books), and would require a stated penalty to be effective, as is the case elsewhere in both the Old Testament and in ancient Near Eastern casuistic law.

In brief, the Decalogue should probably be understood — as it has been throughout subsequent history — as a series of basic principles of conduct, partly religious and partly ethical, which came to be recognized in Israel — possibly fairly late, and perhaps in connection with the didactic "preaching" of the Deuteronomists — as summing up what was essential to Israel's way of life as commanded by God. It may have had its origins in the same way as the much more restricted apodictic code of the Rechabite sect mentioned in Jer. 35:6-7, who are there said to follow the commandments of their ancestor Jonadab, to drink no wine, build no house, sow no seed, and plant no vineyard, but to live in tents. Two prophetic oracles (Hos. 4:2; Jer. 7:9) show a clear knowledge of a group of the ethical principles enunciated in the Decalogue, and regard these as referring to things particularly abhorrent to Yahweh; but there is no way of proving whether these prophets were familiar with the whole of the Decalogue in its final form.

The Book of the Covenant (Exodus 20:22–23:33)

Like the Decalogue, this collection of laws is an originally independent collection that has been inserted into its present context and so brought into connection with the making of the covenant on Sinai. The laws themselves comprise 20:22–23:19, the final verses (23:20-33) being a parenetic addition. Casuistic and apodictic laws are to some extent mixed together, but it should be noted that, while the casuistic laws constitute the central section, the apodictic laws are mainly grouped together at the beginning and the end (20:23-26; 23:9-19).

The apodictic laws here, although they include regulations of a more general kind, are characteristically Yahwistic in that they forbid the making of divine images and the worship of other gods than Yahweh. They also include laws concerning the making and use of altars presumably dedicated to Yahweh and laws concerning clearly Yahwistic religious observances: sacrifice, the three peculiarly Yahwistic feasts, and the sabbath. If the "participial" laws carrying the death penalty are counted as apodictic, these laws repeat no less than four provisions of the Decalogue which occur in the immediately preceding chapter, concerning the avoidance of the worship of other gods, murder, behavior toward parents, and the observance of the sabbath.

The casuistic laws, however, have no such specifically Yahwistic character. Although they are not arranged in strictly logical order, they may be roughly classified as follows:

21:1-11   Laws regulating the treatment of slaves, particularly "humanitarian" provisions

21:12-17 Laws carrying the death penalty (if these are to be seen as casuistic): homicide, behavior toward parents, kidnapping

21:18-36 Laws concerning bodily injuries

22:1-16   Laws concerning damage to property

22:17-28 Miscellaneous laws (including some apodictic laws)

23:1-9   Laws concerning the administration of justice and social obligations (including some apodictic laws)

Many of these laws concern matters also dealt with in ancient Near Eastern law codes, although none is identical with any extant non-Israelite law. The affinities with the Near Eastern legal tradition, however, suggest that some dependence on the (presumed) laws of pre-Israelite Canaan is a probability. The view of some scholars that the laws here, or some of them, reflect a presettlement nomadic existence is improbable. They are largely concerned with such matters as the ownership or disputed ownership of farm livestock (which was clearly of great importance), with the growing of crops, with viticulture, with theft from private houses, and with the ownership of domestic slaves — in other words, with a settled mode of agricultural life.

There are few references to religion in the casuistic laws of the Book of the Covenant. There is no reason to suppose that the occasional references to "God" or "the gods" (Hebrew *elohim, ha-elohim* in Exod. 21:6, 13; 22:9, 28) originally had Yahweh in mind. The three occurrences of the name Yahweh are in apodictic, not casuistic, laws, and belong to a later Yahwistic redaction.

The final redaction may have taken place when the Book of the Covenant was placed in its present position; but the combination of the specifically Yahwistic, apodictic laws with the casuistic ones may well be of an earlier date, when this was still an independent document.

The date of its final composition is impossible to determine. All that can be affirmed is that the Book of the Covenant cannot be earlier than Israel's first close contact, as resident in the land, with the Canaanites, nor obviously earlier than the adoption of the religion of Yahweh by the Israelites. Also, it must have been earlier than the composition of the laws of Deuteronomy, which show a clear dependence on it. Since Israelite law, though perhaps imposed by kings during the time of the monarchy, was not "royal law" in the sense of having been made by kings, the absence of any references to kings, or indeed to any centralized government, does not necessarily imply that it is premonarchic.

The Laws of Deuteronomy

Some aspects of these laws have already been discussed in chapter 6 above. It is clear that in some respects they are an "improved" version of the Book of the Covenant; they presuppose, rephrase, and to some extent interpret and adapt many of the earlier laws. The two collections thus overlap in subject matter to a considerable extent, and Deuteronomy has retained the casuistic form in appropriate cases; but the apodictic form is much more prominent here. The Deuteronomic laws, unlike those of the Book of the Covenant, were from the outset wholly designed to set forth a series of obligations imposed unconditionally on the covenant people. In many cases the older laws have been expanded to give more precise instructions on particular subjects, and also to take account of the circumstances and requirements of a more developed society. For example, the laws of Exod. 21:12-14 about homicide have been expanded into a much longer set of provisions in Deut. 19:4-13, which provide among other things for the legal protection of those who commit unintentional homicides. In Deut. 16:18–20:20 there is generally a much more extended treatment of the administration of justice and of national institutions and officials — king, priests, prophets — together with laws on the conduct of war. But like the laws of the Book of the Covenant, the Deuteronomic laws do not provide for every contingency for which modern state law would be expected to provide (although to some extent they are intended to limit the discretionary powers of the local courts of elders). They are not a complete statutory code that would have been consulted by either local or nationally appointed judges in every case. Nor do the laws follow any clear logical arrangement, although attempts have been made by some scholars (e.g.,

Calum M. Carmichael) to discover some kind of scheme or arrangement. Some laws, however, are roughly grouped together by topic: for example, Deut. 12:1–16:17 are mainly concerned with worship, and 16:18–18:22 with official leaders and institutions. From ch. 21 on no particular arrangement is evident. The lack of obvious arrangement may be partly due to additions that have been made to the original collection, which itself has incorporated a number of groups on particular topics that once had a separate existence.

The most original, and indeed revolutionary, feature of the Deuteronomic legislation is to be found in the laws concerning worship. These are most clearly set out in ch. 12. This chapter orders the destruction of all the places at which worship has previously been offered, and commands that public (sacrificial) worship is to be practiced only in one place, "the place that Yahweh your God will choose out of all your tribes to put his name there" (vv. 5, 11, 14, 18). As has been pointed out, this is a major innovation. The Covenant Code speaks of permitted worship at "every place where I cause my name to be remembered" (Exod. 20:24); and, as is well known, the preexilic literature testifies to the existence of many places in the land at which worship was legitimately offered, although some of the prophets had condemned the kind of worship which was practiced at some of these. Whatever may have been the connection of this law with the religious reforms of Josiah (see chapter 6 above), its purpose was to ensure that all worship should be carried out in accordance with what the Deuteronomic legislators considered to be the will of God. The one sanctuary was the outward expression of purity of worship and, indeed, of purity of life as envisaged by the Deuteronomists. The law of the single sanctuary marked a crucial and long-lasting change in the religious practice of Israel.

The moralistic, preaching tone characteristic of the book (see chapter 6 above) is not confined to the more obviously sermonlike chs. 1-11 but pervades the laws as well. Although what are known as "motive clauses" — subordinate clauses attached to particular laws justifying them or explaining the reason for them — occur already in the Book of the Covenant, they occur with particular frequency in the laws of Deuteronomy. Berend Gemser in his seminal study of the question estimated that whereas the proportion of laws in the Book of the Covenant provided with motive clauses is 17 percent, in Deuteronomy it is 60 percent. The motive clause, which is apparently a peculiarity of Israelite law — it is not found in any extant ancient Near Eastern law code according to Gemser — may be of various kinds. In Deuteronomy it is overwhelmingly religious and/or ethical, mainly intended to remind readers of Yahweh's actions on their behalf in the past — of the state of misery in Egypt from which he had rescued his people, of the covenant which he had established with them, and of his gift to them of the land which they are about to occupy.

As has already been noted, Deuteronomy has a unique literary style which is unmistakable even when translated into other languages. This is mainly because it repeats, with slight variations, characteristic phrases which express its theological point of view (see the list in S. R. Driver, *Introduction to the Literature of the Old Testament*).

References to worship at "the place that Yahweh your God shall choose to put his name there" are especially frequent. Also frequent are references to the former slavery of the people in Egypt and Yahweh's rescue of them. There are fourteen references to Egypt in these laws; several of them (Deut. 15:15; 24:18, 22) are attached as motive clauses to laws commanding just and humane treatment of slaves, orphans, and widows. Others lay particular stress on the necessity to preserve the purity of the community that Yahweh has redeemed (13:5, 10), or express thanksgiving for that redemption (26:5, 8).

It may be thought strange that the final editor of the Pentateuch should have preserved two major sets of laws that to a large extent cover the same ground (the Book of the Covenant and Deuteronomy), of which Deuteronomy is partly a revision and expansion and even a correction of the older collection and has a much more explicit theology. There may have been several reasons for this.

Clearly the Deuteronomist did not regard the laws of Deuteronomy as superseding the Book of the Covenant. There are in fact fewer contradictions between the two than has often been supposed. The main apparent inconsistency concerns the question of whether more than one place of worship was to be permitted; and even here it is not clear that Exod. 20:24 was *understood* as contrary to the law of Deut. 12. Although it may have been the *intention* of Exod. 20:24 that multiple places of sacrifice were to be tolerated, the text does not actually state that this is the case. This is in fact suggested only by a single Hebrew word, *kol-*, presumed to mean "every," and this word is missing in the Samaritan version of the Pentateuch, which reads "in *the* place."

The duplication of earlier laws in Deuteronomy is not an isolated phenomenon in the Pentateuch. It has already been pointed out above that several of the laws in the Book of the Covenant duplicate some of the commandments of the Decalogue, and there are many other such duplications elsewhere in the Pentateuch (e.g., between the Decalogue, the "Ritual Decalogue" of Exod. 34:14-26, and the Book of the Covenant). This phenomenon may be partly based on the principle that repetition can be an effective means of drawing attention to what is being said and of impressing its importance on the persons addressed. But in the case of the Pentateuch, it may also be due to what Samuel Sandmel called "a disinclination to expunge" ("The Haggada Within Scripture," 120).

Sandmel's main concern was with the narrative parts of the Pentateuch and with putting forward an alternative to the Documentary Hypothesis, but his observations are equally applicable to the laws. He used an analogy from the practice of the later Jewish haggadah, in which writers recast biblical stories, embellishing, elaborating, and reinterpreting or correcting them — even after they had been accepted as canonical — without intending in any way to supersede them or to detract from them, but rather to provide a commentary on them. This he called "a literature which grew by accretion" (p. 122). It may well have been this reverence for earlier laws which had been presented as having divine and Mosaic authority that moved these later Pentateuchal writers to preserve them, even though they regarded them as inadequate or incomplete and needing revision. The same applies to the priestly legislation of the Pentateuch to be discussed in the final section of this chapter. This priestly legislation has been generally recognized since the time of Julius Wellhausen to be itself an example of a "literature of accretion," an original set of laws having been augmented over a period of time by insertion into the text of new laws and new clauses which modify, or even sometimes contradict, the original text in haggadic fashion.

The Priestly Laws

Most of the considerable body of laws in the Pentateuch has been appropriately dubbed "priestly." Although often referred to as the "Priestly Code," it is not a compact body of laws gathered into one place, but is to be found scattered through three of the books: Exodus, Leviticus (where it comprises almost the entire book), and Numbers. It is attributed to P by those who accept the Documentary Hypothesis and also by many who have retained the notion of a P document though not the whole of that hypothesis, and is therefore generally held to be postexilic in date. Recently, however, both the attribution and the date have been called into question. Although there are some affinities, both linguistic and theological, between these laws and some of the narratives attributed to P (see chapter 2 above), the laws are best studied, like the other Pentateuchal collections of laws, as having had a separate origin from the narratives in which they are now set.

The priestly laws are mainly unconnected with the other collections of laws in the Pentateuch — they are neither revisions of earlier laws now extant, nor can they be said to have been subject, except internally, to any inner-Pentateuchal revision. In terms of the topics dealt with, their scope is infinitely more restricted than that of either the Book of the Covenant or Deuteronomy. Although like the other collections they are mainly represented as having been addressed, with some exceptions, to the whole people through the medium of Moses (and Aaron) at Sinai, in reality the matters with which they deal are matters of particular interest to the priesthood rather than to the laity: matters concerning priestly functions such as the design and construction of the tabernacle in the wilderness, the proper procedures for the offering of the various types of sacrifice, the anointing and vestments of Aaron and his sons as priests, rules about edible and forbidden animals, physical impurities and leprosy, the rules for the observance of the Day of Atonement, and the regulations for the observance of the major festivals. Although many of these rules, such as the actual slaughter of the sacrificial animals and the food laws, were to be carried out by laypersons, it was the priests whose duty it was to see that they were properly performed.

Nowhere else in the Pentateuch are the details of sacrificial and other rites set out. The cultic rules of the Book of the Covenant are restricted to a few brief references mainly to the altar, the sabbath, and the observance of the festivals without giving any details. Deuteronomy also, apart from its emphasis on the importance of the restriction of sacrificial worship to a single place, is equally unconcerned with its details. The only part of the priestly legislation that has substantial affinities with the other collections of laws in the Pentateuch is the so-called Holiness Code (H), Lev. 17-26. This has marked characteristics of its own (see below).

There is a limited sense, then, in which the priestly laws, or at any rate their central body, the book of Leviticus, could be called a handbook for the use of the priests which was at some later time made public. But in fact it is both less and more than that. Like all Pentateuchal legislation, despite careful attention to detail the priestly laws fall far short of giving a complete description of the cultic acts to which they refer. There is no mention, for example, of *texts* or fixed forms of words which might have accompanied the sacrifices. It is not known what words may have been recited, for example, or whether psalms may have been sung — though many of the extant psalms in the Psalter appear to be very appropriate for such occasions. We really have no clear idea of the daily round of worship that was practiced at the temple. Some later Jewish texts, written after the final destruction of the Jerusalem temple in A.D. 70, give some additional details, and these may have preserved some memories of what had taken place, but it is not possible to be certain of their reliability. Much of the detailed regulations for worship was presumably kept in oral form, handed down by one generation of priests to the next while the temple(s) lasted. But the absence of information makes it impossible to construct a *history* of temple worship, which — though the tradition was probably very conservative and only changed slowly — must have undergone considerable changes over the centuries as a result of the cultic reforms initiated from time to time by the kings of Judah and above all the reestablishment of the temple after the Exile. Our lack of knowledge about these things also makes it extremely difficult to know what period or periods are represented by the priestly laws which we have in the Pentateuch.

It is easy for modern readers to dismiss the priestly laws as an unimportant or uncharacteristic side of Israel's religion, as representing a cruder or more mechanical, legalistic conception of human relations with the deity than the teaching of the prophets, for example — or simply as extremely tedious reading! This view has been fostered by the dominant influence of Wellhausen, who regarded the teaching of the "classical" prophets with its "ethical monotheism" as the high point of the Israelite faith, which had been followed by a steep decline especially in the postexilic period. Wellhausen said of the priestly sacrificial system, "The warm pulse of life no longer throbbed in it to animate it; it was no longer the blossom and the fruit of every branch of life. . . . The soul was fled; the shell remained, upon the shaping out of which every energy was now concentrated. A manifoldness of rites took the place of individualising occasions; technique was the main thing, and strict fidelity to rubric" (*Prolegomena to the History of Ancient Israel,* 78). This dismissive view has been perpetuated in treatments of the subject which until very recent times, like other aspects of Old Testament study, have been dominated by liberal Protestants for whom set forms of worship were contrary to their free spirit, and who had no understanding or appreciation of their underlying religious and theological value.

Before considering the validity of this judgment on the priestly laws, it is important to take into account some recent discussion of the hitherto dominant consensus about their antiquity. Wellhausen in his *Prolegomena* mainly derived his late dating of these laws from a comparison with the scattered information in the preexilic literature of the Old Testament about the practice of sacrificial worship. He did not, however, take sufficient account of the fact that this literature does not purport to give a precise account of sacrifice, but refers to it mainly in passing; even the earlier collections of laws give very few details. The priestly laws are the first — and indeed the only — formal account of the practice in the Old Testament. It is important to realize that they are written from a particular perspective quite different from those of the other books — that is, from the *professional* point of view of the priesthood, which was also the audience for which they were originally intended.

An even more important point is that Wellhausen did not take into account — and was in fact not able to take into account at the time when he wrote — the mass of documents from the ancient Near East which shows that the priestly laws of sacrifice were not a late Jewish invention but are in many respects characteristic of ancient Near Eastern practice many centuries earlier than the Old Testament. The complexity and meticulous attention to detail of sacrificial legislation were central features of the ancient Near East of which Israel was a part. That the significance of this has only recently been realized, and only by a few scholars, is surprising. The shadow cast by Wellhausen is a long one.

That these laws may contain *some* material that is older than the now conventional exilic or postexilic date has long been surmised by some scholars. But it was the Jewish scholar Yehezkel Kaufmann (1930) who first argued against Wellhausen that the whole collection is preexilic and presents none of the features characteristic of the Jerusalem community of the postexilic period. More recently other Jewish scholars (Avi Hurvitz, Menahem Haran, and Jacob Milgrom) have pursued the question further in general agreement with Kaufmann. Hurvitz confined himself to a study of the language of the priestly laws, and showed by a comparison of this with the language of Ezekiel, Chronicles, and Ezra-Nehemiah — books also much concerned with cultic matters and all written in a Hebrew later than the "classical" Hebrew of the preexilic period — that the priestly laws of the Pentateuch show no knowledge of the priestly terminology employed in those books, but conform linguistically to the Hebrew of the preexilic ("First Temple") period.

Haran reviewed the history of the priestly functions and institutions as far as this is possible, and on the basis of that investigation also came to the conclusion that the priestly legislation "derives from conditions that prevailed in the pre-exilic, not the post-exilic, period of ancient Israelite history" (*Temples and Temple-Service in Ancient Israel*, v). He accounts for the fact that this legislation apparently had no influence on communal life until the time of Ezra on the grounds that it was an esoteric work closely guarded by the small circle of priests and not known to the general public until then. Strangely, however, Haran does not deal with the difficulty, frequently used as an argument for a postexilic date, that two types of sacrifice, the "sin offering" (Hebrew *hattat*) and "guilt offering" *(asham)* — which play a prominent part in the priestly sacrificial system and were public sacrifices — are hardly mentioned, if at all, in the preexilic literature. (These terms are also not dealt with by Hurvitz; Milgrom uses the fact that they are virtually confined to the priestly laws to prove that the laws are *early*, later superseded by other terms before the Exile; *Leviticus 1-16*, 177.)

Since it has been established by comparison with the practices of other Near Eastern peoples that a complex system of priestly legislation *could* have developed in Israel at a comparatively early date, it remains to consider the possibilities with regard to the general nature of the biblical material itself. The conventional view is that the legislation is the work of the Israelite priesthood either during its exile in Babylonia, when it could not be put into practice but could make sense as a "blueprint" for future use in the hoped-for restored Jerusalem temple (possibly like the "laws" of Ezek. 40-48), or shortly afterwards when the Second Temple was being, or had just been, built. But the nature and complexity of the material make this highly improbable. Such complex systems are not created "from scratch"; old traditions would surely not have simply been ignored. At the least, it may be assumed that these laws can only have been based on memories of the system that had actually been in use just before the destruction of the First Temple. This makes it extremely probable that what we now have here, however much it may have been altered and expanded at a later time, is basically the traditional lore and practice of the temple built by Solomon which had no doubt developed and been modified over a long period during the following centuries. However old some of it may have been — Milgrom suggests that it contains laws which go back beyond Solomon to the ancient Israelite temple at Shiloh — there seems, now that the question has been considered anew, no reason to doubt that it is substantially the priestly laws of the preexilic period.

Like most legislation, the priestly laws provide little direct information about their raison d'être. Especially in contrast to Deuteronomy, which is an exception to the rule, there are very few statements here of an overtly theological nature. Nevertheless, that there is a significant underlying theology that gives meaning to the whole cannot be denied.

Various attempts have been made to identify a central theological theme. Perhaps the concept of divinely established *order* is that which best accounts for the multiplicity of matters with which the laws are concerned. Behind them lies the concept of God as a God of order, and of the world as an ordered creation which, in as far as it has departed from that order, needs to be restored to it by means that God himself has provided for its restoration. Such an essentially static notion of a divinely established norm to which everything ought to conform in harmony is characteristic of the priesthoods of other religious systems as well.

This concern with order manifests itself in many ways. One of these is the great insistence on atonement for sin in the priestly laws. It was the aim of the sacrificial laws of the sin offering and guilt offering to restore the sinner and so to reestablish a normal state of affairs in society at large. This was not automatically achieved simply by the offering of sacrifice, although that was essential. Most importantly, confession of guilt was required (Lev. 5:5-6). Only in cases of flagrant sin when the sinner "insults Yahweh" and has "brought the word of Yahweh into contempt and violated his command" (REB) was forgiveness not possible: "such a person shall be utterly cut off and bear the guilt" (Num. 15:31).

The need for redemption from the consequences of sin was not, however, simply an individual concern; this was a situation which also involved the whole people (Num. 25-26). That is the reason for the setting aside of one day in the year as a Day of Atonement (Hebrew *yom hakkippurim,* Lev. 23:27) when Aaron and subsequently "the priest who is anointed and consecrated as priest in his father's place" (Lev. 16:32) was to enter the holy place to make atonement for the whole people for all their sins committed in the previous year. Sin was thus a breach of the covenant that God had made with his people which, if it remained unconfessed and unatoned for, would result in their total destruction (Lev. 26:23-45).

The divine ordering of life was not only observable with respect to Israel; it was cosmic in scope. This is well illustrated by the laws concerning the classification of animals into two groups: those which were permitted, and those which were forbidden, to be eaten (Lev. 11; a similar list appears in Deut. 14:3-20). This clearly implies God's ordering of the whole of the natural world. Many attempts have been made to discover a rational, or even a theological, basis for these distinctions between the kinds of animals; they have particularly interested anthropologists. No consensus, however, has been reached on this question. The explanation given in the text is simply that the people are commanded to "make a distinction between the unclean and the clean" (Lev. 11:47). Such distinctions between clean and unclean, and also between holy and profane, are an extremely prominent feature of the priestly laws (see Lev. 10:10-11 for a general command given to Aaron). They all testify to the concern for the divine order in life, as also does the insistence on the distinction between the respective functions of the priesthood and the laity, the overstepping of which could be fatal. Yahweh was to be worshipped only in the prescribed way and in prescribed places.

The Tabernacle. In Exod. 25-30 Moses is told to make a large structure called a *mishkan* (the usual English translation is "tabernacle") and the various items of furniture for it. Chs. 35-40 report the execution of those directives. These chapters also contain an instruction to anoint Aaron and his sons to serve as priests and a corresponding account of its execution. The tabernacle was to be carried about by the Levites, to accompany the Israelites during the remainder of their journey through the desert; and they were to guard it from the approach of "outsiders," the penalty for which was death (Num. 1:50-51). When the work was completed it is recorded that the tabernacle was filled with the appearance of Yahweh's glory, signifying his approval and presence.

Much has been written about these chapters. One thing that is agreed is that the tabernacle is an ideal rather than a historical phenomenon; that such a massive structure could have been built and carried for many years through the desert is an obvious impossibility. These chapters are an extreme example of a persistent tendency of the Pentateuchal writers to assert that all later religious institutions were founded at Sinai, at the very beginning of Israelite history, through the mediation of Moses himself. The tabernacle as described here is clearly a model for the Jerusalem temple of the future. It does not correspond exactly to either Solomon's temple or the postexilic temple, though it does so in many of its details. An important article of its furniture is the ark of the covenant, which no longer existed in postexilic times.

It is stated in Exod. 25:9, 40 that the model, or pattern (Hebrew *tabhnith*), according to which the tabernacle and its furnishings were to be constructed had been shown to Moses by God when he stood in God's presence on Mount Sinai. This is another example of the concern of the priestly laws for the divine ordering of the whole of Israel's life in the smallest detail. But the chief importance of the tabernacle is theological. It symbolizes the presence of Yahweh with his people wherever they go and the importance of the distinction between the holy and the profane (in this case with regard to holy places), as well as the centrality of the temple in Israel's religious life.

The Holiness Code. Leviticus 17-26 has been called the Holiness Code because of the frequency of the occurrence of the phrase, attributed to Yahweh: "You shall be holy because I am holy," which corresponds to the theological theme of the other priestly laws but here receives a special emphasis. One other phrase is characteristic of these chapters: "I am Yahweh" (sometimes "I am Yahweh your God"). It is generally believed that these chapters originally constituted an independent collection of laws that has been subsequently inserted into the main body of Leviticus. There can be no doubt that they emanate from the same general circles as the other priestly laws, but their standpoint is slightly different.

The order in which these laws have been arranged is far from obvious. They are a mixture of laws on a variety of different subjects. Many of them virtually repeat the substance of laws that occur elsewhere in the Pentateuch, but there are a number of minor details in which they differ from the other priestly laws. The collection also contains a substantial number of laws about the conduct of ordinary life that resemble the Book of the Covenant or Deuteronomy rather than Leviticus. This collection concludes, like Deut. 28, with blessings and curses.

For Further Reading

Alt, Albrecht. "The Origins of Israelite Law," in *Essays on Old Testament History and Religion*. Oxford: Blackwell, 1966, and Garden City: Doubleday, 1968, 79-132. Repr. Sheffield: JSOT Press, 1989. (First published in German, 1940.)

Blenkinsopp, Joseph. *The Pentateuch: An Introduction to the First Five Books of the Bible*. New York: Doubleday and London: SCM, 1992, ch. 6.

Boecker, Hans-Jochen. *Law and the Administration of Justice in the Old Testament and the Ancient East.* Minneapolis: Augsburg and London: SPCK, 1980. (First published in German, 1976.)

Carmichael, Calum M. *The Laws of Deuteronomy.* Ithaca: Cornell University Press, 1974.

Cody, Aelred. *A History of Old Testament Priesthood.* Analecta Biblica 35. Rome: Pontifical Biblical Institute Press, 1969.

Douglas, Mary. *In the Wilderness: The Doctrine of Defilement in the Book of Numbers.* JSOT Supplement 158. Sheffield: JSOT Press, 1993.

Gemser, Berend. "The Importance of the Motive Clause in Old Testament Law," VTS 1. Leiden: Brill, 1953, 50-66.

Grabbe, Lester L. *Leviticus.* OTG. Sheffield: JSOT Press, 1993.

Haran, Menahem. "Behind the Scenes of History: Determining the Date of the Priestly Source," *JBL* 100 (1981): 321-333.

————. *Temples and Temple-Service in Ancient Israel.* Oxford: Clarendon Press, 1978.

Houston, Walter. *Purity and Monotheism: Clean and Unclean Animals in Biblical Law.* JSOT Supplement 140. Sheffield: JSOT Press, 1993.

Hurvitz, Avi. "The Evidence of Language in Dating the Priestly Code," *RB* 81 (1974): 24-56.

Levine, Baruch A. *Numbers 1-20.* AB 4. New York: Doubleday, 1993.

Mendenhall, George E. "Ancient Oriental and Biblical Law," *BA* 17 (1954): 26-46. Repr. in *The BA Reader* 3, ed. E. F. Campbell, Jr., and David Noel Freedman. Garden City: Doubleday, 1970, 3-24.

Mettinger, T. N. D. *The Dethronement of Sabaoth.* Coniectanea Biblica, Old Testament 18. Lund: Gleerup, 1982.

Milgrom, Jacob. *Leviticus 1-16.* AB 3. New York: Doubleday, 1991.

Nielsen, Eduard. *The Ten Commandments in New Perspective.* SBT, 2nd Series 7. Naperville: Allenson and London: SCM, 1968. (First published in German, 1965.)

Noth, Martin. "The Laws in the Pentateuch: Their Assumptions and Meaning," in *The Laws in the Pentateuch and Other Studies.* Edinburgh: London: Oliver & Boyd, 1966, and Philadephia: Fortress, 1967, 1-107. Repr. London: SCM, 1984. (Translated from the 2nd German ed., 1960.)

————. *Leviticus.* OTL. Philadelphia: Westminster and London: SCM, 1965. Rev. ed., 1977. (First published in German, 1962.)

Paul, Shalom M. *Studies in the Book of the Covenant in the Light of Cuneiform and Biblical Law.* VTS 18. Leiden: Brill, 1970.

Phillips, Anthony. *Ancient Israel's Criminal Law: A New Approach to the Decalogue*. New York: Schocken and Oxford: Blackwell, 1970.

Rowley, H. H. "Moses and the Decalogue," in *Men of God: Studies in Old Testament History and Prophecy*. London: Nelson, 1963, 1-36. (First published 1951-52.)

Sandmel, Samuel, "The Haggada Within Scripture," *JBL* 80 (1961): 105-122.

Stamm, J. J., and Andrew, M. E. *The Ten Commandments in Recent Research*. SBT, 2nd Series 2. Naperville: Allenson and London: SCM, 1967. (Includes additions from the 2nd German ed., 1962.)

Wellhausen, Julius. *Prolegomena to the History of Ancient Israel*. Edinburgh: A. & C. Binck, 1885. Repr. Magnolia, Mass.: Peter Smith, 1977. (First published in German, 1878.)

Westbrook, Raymond. "Biblical and Cuneiform Law Codes," *RB* 92 (1985): 247-264.

CHAPTER 8

Reading the Pentateuch

THERE ARE A NUMBER of different ways of reading the Pentateuch. Since it is basically a single continuous narrative into which laws and poems have been inserted at appropriate points, it can be read simply as an account of the origin and early history of the people of Israel, preceded by a more general section dealing with the creation of the world and the earliest period of human history. It cannot be doubted that, among other things, this is what the Pentateuch purported to be — what it was in the eyes of those who produced it in its present form. As such it is similar in many ways to the accounts that other peoples have given of their origins.

The Pentateuch may also be read simply as literature; and on this level also it may be compared with other literatures. This approach has taken several forms. For example, form criticism, initiated by Hermann Gunkel, has studied the individual stories in Genesis, and to some extent those of Exodus and Numbers, as examples of "saga," that is, as originally independent short stories; longer sections such as the story of Joseph have been taken as more elaborate examples of the short "novel," of which again other examples are to be found in ancient Near Eastern literatures. Much attention has also been paid to the structure of the narrative and legal material and indeed of whole books (e.g., Mary Douglas). The narratives have been investigated as examples of refined and subtle writing (e.g., Robert Alter). These scholars have demonstrated that the Pentateuch as a whole is indeed an astonishing literary achievement.

The Pentateuch has also been studied from the perspective of the comparative study of religions. The religious customs attributed to the patriarchs of Genesis and to the age of Moses have been compared with those of other ancient Near Eastern peoples; and a voluminous literature has been produced along these lines, comparing for example the accounts of the creation of the world and the other narratives of Gen. 1-11 with the mythologies of the ancient world.

The Pentateuchal laws, which account for about one-half of the material, have been studied not only by comparing the various groups of biblical laws with one another, but also by comparing them with the substantial body of extant legal codes from the ancient Near East, so revealing many affinities with these as well as significant differences.

It has also been supposed that the Pentateuch offers important evidence concerning the development of Israelite religion over the centuries. This enterprise went hand in hand with the view that the material which comprises the Pentateuch originated in different historical periods, and that it is possible to discover the relative, if not the absolute, ages of different parts of it and to link this with what is known from elsewhere in the Old Testament of the developing religion of Israel. This was the presupposition, and also the fruit, of the source criticism of proponents of the Documentary Hypothesis which was also in its own right one of the principal approaches made to the study of the Pentateuch. This attempt to trace religious development in the Pentateuch has not, however, been confined to "classical" source criticism.

Archaeology has also had its part to play in the study of the Pentateuch. Archaeologists have contributed to the identification of some of the many places mentioned in these books, for example, stopping places on the route of the Israelites from Egypt to Palestine. Ancient Near Eastern texts discovered by archaeologists have also been used in attempts to locate the historical setting and date of the patriarchs and of Israel's sojourn in Egypt, though it has since been shown that much of the supposed evidence in question is in fact invalid and that the quest itself is misconceived (see Thomas L. Thompson).

The above list of approaches to the Pentateuch is by no means exhaustive. Among others that deserve special mention are the geographical (e.g., in considering the location of the crossing of the Sea), the sociological, and the anthropological (e.g., in the study of the social setting and family customs of the patriarchs). Each has its own value, although in some cases this is a negative one. Two important aspects of reading these books, however, remain to be considered: the intention and meaning of the Pentateuch in its final form in the minds of those who were responsible for its composition, and its meaning and message for today. The second of these, though obviously of paramount importance, lies outside the scope of this book. It is a theological matter; moreover, it is not a subject for the study of the Pentateuch alone, but one which pertains to the theological study of the Old Testament as a whole. The first, however, is that which I have chosen to follow in this book as my main approach to the Pentateuch.

This approach, which characterizes especially chapters 3-5 above, is what is today known as "synchronic." That is, the Pentateuch in its final form is treated as a "book" which exists in its own right as an artifact with a theme and a message. This approach is distinct from the "diachronic," which is concerned primarily with the history of composition, which may (or may not) have extended over a long period. It has not, however, been possible to use the synchronic approach consistently in the treatment of Deuteronomy or of the laws, since in both these cases a consideration of historical origins and subsequent developments is necessary in order to explain the motives and intentions of those who composed this material. Moreover, the indications of different stages of composition are clearer in Deuteronomy and the laws than in the narrative sections, and the techniques used were different from those used in the narratives. Nevertheless, the diachronic method has been avoided as much as possible here as well.

The advantage of using the synchronic approach is that in this way one is dealing with something concrete that actually exists: the text of the Pentateuch, which lies before us. The diachronic method is necessarily speculative. It is an attempt to discover earlier "texts" lying below the surface, whether written or oral, which may have existed at various times and which are supposed to have been subsequently incorporated into the present text — often in a greatly changed form and to serve new purposes — and to postulate historical situations in the history and religious history of Israel in which they may have arisen. These earlier "versions" do not actually exist; they are simply postulated.

For a long time, since the work of Julius Wellhausen, there was a general consensus about the identity of these sources — though there has always been some disagreement over details, and there have always been some scholars who did not accept the Documentary Hypothesis. But now the consensus has broken down; and the complete lack of agreement at the present time about the composition of the Pentateuch should warn the student that theories about the dates of different parts of it are extremely subjective.

Another circumstance affecting the present-day study of the Pentateuch is that there is now great uncertainty about the history of the religion of Israel, especially the earlier stages which were closely linked to theories about sources. A diachronic method is therefore much more difficult to sustain now than before. It must be admitted that the view taken in this book about the late date of the Pentateuch — exilic or immediately post-exilic — is also to some extent subjective. It cannot be proved beyond possibility of doubt that it was designed to fit such a situation. But dating it is in fact a secondary issue. What is much more important is to see the Pentateuch as a (relatively) consistent whole with its own overriding theme.

This primary theme, as has been amply demonstrated above, is undoubtedly that of the promises made to the patriarchs from Abraham on. By the end of Deuteronomy these have to a large extent been fulfilled: here is a great and powerful people, living under the (admittedly conditional) blessing of God. Yet, although Israel is poised to enter the Promised Land, this final fulfillment of the promises has not yet been achieved. Even the casual reader who regards the Pentateuch as a self-contained entity and does not go on to read the book of Joshua will be inclined to ask why. The answer to this question probably lies in the process by which the books of the Old Testament were assembled in their present order. Unfortunately the mechanics of this process are by no means clear to us.

It is only when the Pentateuch is regarded as a closed entity that this problem of the non-fulfillment, or partial fulfillment, of the promises arises. The reader who comes to the Bible without any presuppositions about the Torah's being a work quite separate from the succeeding books will find an unbroken story line in the whole complex of Genesis to Kings, from the creation of the world to the fall of the kingdom of Judah in the early sixth century B.C. He or she will read straight through the division that now exists between Deuteronomy and the book of Joshua, noting that although the anointing of Joshua as Moses' successor and the report of Moses' death at the end of Deuteronomy clearly mark the end of an era and the beginning of a new one, Joshua begins quite naturally as a resumption of the narrative: "After the death of Moses . . . the Lord spoke to Joshua" (Josh. 1:1). The very next verse moves the story on, with Yahweh's words: "My servant Moses is dead. Now proceed to cross the Jordan, you and all this people, into the land that I am giving them." There is no break in the narrative. Even the language used is the same as in Deuteronomy.

This does not necessarily mean, as some scholars have maintained in the past, that the first books of the Old Testament originally formed a "Hexateuch" or group of six — that Joshua, which completes the fulfillment of the promises, was originally an integral part of this group of books which subsequently became detached from the others because it does not belong to the Mosaic era (e.g., S. R. Driver, *Introduction to the Literature of the Old Testament*, 5-6, 103; contrast Martin Noth, *A History of Pentateuchal Traditions*, 6). The current view that, on the contrary, the books of Joshua, Judges, Samuel, and Kings together with Deuteronomy form a distinct work, the so-called Deuteronomistic History, works in the opposite direction, reducing the "Pentateuch" to a "Tetrateuch" (a group of four books).

The question of the relationship of Deuteronomy to the rest of the Pentateuch on the one hand and to Joshua and the following books on the other remains problematic. It is possible that more than one way of dividing these books was adopted at different times, operating in different directions. An attractive solution to the problem, offered by A. D. H. Mayes (*The Story of Israel between Settlement and Exile*, 139-149, especially 141) on the basis of a suggestion by Rolf Rendtorff (*The Problem of the Process of Transmission in the Pentateuch*, 200), is that the Deuteronomistic History (perhaps in an early edition) was formed first, and that the Pentateuch, which had not previously existed (at any rate as a distinct work) was composed somewhat later as an *introduction* to it. This would account for the absence in the Pentateuch of a full account of the settlement of the Israelites in Canaan. The Deuteronomistic History, or rather the narrative part of it, begins with its account of the settlement. There was therefore no need for the composer of the Pentateuch to repeat this. His function was to take the story *up to* the entry into Canaan; and he joined his work to the opening verses of the book of Joshua with his account of the immediately preceding events, the anointing of Joshua and the death of Moses. This is probably a better account of the matter than, for example, Noth's hypothesis that a full account of the settlement originally stood in the Pentateuch but was subsequently truncated in order to allow room for the account in Joshua (*A History of Pentateuchal Traditions*, 71-74).

The view that the Pentateuch was composed as an introduction to the Deuteronomistic History is a plausible one. The Deuteronomistic work was conceived as a history of the Israelite people from their settlement in Canaan to the fall of the kingdom of Judah. It is claimed that this was then supplemented by an introductory section which, in the manner of some other ancient national histories, was concerned to make certain specific claims about Israel's most remote origins, laying particular emphasis on the nation as especially chosen and guided by God toward the achievement of a great destiny in the land of Canaan under the divine blessing. This introduction — the Pentateuch — showed how Israel or its patriarchal ancestors had been delivered by God on a number of occasions from apparently inevitable destruction, but especially from slavery and the murderous intentions of the Egyptian ruler and again, after its departure from Egypt, by the miracle at the Sea — a deliverance that would remain in the minds of the readers and give them encouragement to persevere also in later times of oppression and disaster. The further provision in the opening chapters of Genesis of stories about the creation of the world and the behavior of the earliest human beings, and the linking of this "primeval history" to the ancestors of Israel by a series of genealogies are not uncommon features of such works.

That the Pentateuch bears the marks of the same "school" of writers and editors as the Deuteronomistic History has now been widely recognized; the lapse of time between the composition of the two may have been quite short. As has been suggested above, the period into which such a work most plausibly fits is either that which followed the destruction of the kingdom of Judah in 587 or the early postexilic period when the Jerusalem community was attempting, among renewed difficulties, to reestablish itself. Both works, the Pentateuch and the Deuteronomistic History, are didactic, concerned to inculcate a variety of lessons to their readers.

The lessons that the Pentateuchal author(s) were concerned to teach their readers are numerous; they are by no means confined to the theme of the promises and their fulfillment. The figure of Moses, which dominates the whole work from Exodus on and gives these books their literary and religious unity, is clearly presented as an example of faithfulness and obedience to the divine will and to the mission which had been entrusted to him. It has been said that Moses is essentially a royal figure — a model of the ideal ruler. He embodies virtually all the qualities of leadership that are to be found elsewhere in the Old Testament. It is he who creates a nation out of a confused, helpless, and often rebellious rabble. Moses is at once its organizer, its guide, its counselor, and its military commander. But he is also the one who is close to God, God's spokesman, the mediator between God and the people, and their intercessor. He promulgates God's laws. Moses is the supreme prophet, and also performs actions usually associated with the priesthood, though it is Aaron who normally performs priestly functions.

Yet Moses is not portrayed as a hero in the usual sense of that term. The principal actor throughout the Pentateuch is always God. Moses is

God's servant, but on many occasions the author makes a point of presenting him as a fallible human being. At the outset Moses runs away after killing the Egyptian (Exod. 2:11-15). Later he is full of self-doubt, believing himself to be unfit for the task of facing Pharaoh and leading the people out of Egypt, making various excuses to avoid the task which God sets him, and pleading for someone else to go in his place — and, it is implied, afraid for his life. Even after he has accepted his commission Moses exhibits human weakness. He is prone to violent outbursts of anger; he even expresses dissatisfaction with the position in which God has placed him; and he is capable of direct resistance to God's commands. In the end, although Moses is the object of an enthusiastic encomium (Deut. 34:10-12), his disobedience has earned him a divine displeasure so marked that he is condemned to die without witnessing the fulfillment of his life's work, entry into the Promised Land. There is clearly a warning here that even the most outstanding of God's servants ultimately fall short of what God demands of them. The message that underlies these passages is surely that in the end it is God alone — not even his appointed leaders — who can be trusted.

The *people of Israel* are portrayed in the narratives of Exodus and Numbers as almost continually rebellious. Despite their solemn promises to do all that Yahweh commanded (Exod. 19:8; 24:3), they evince a basic lack of trust in him and in Moses, frequently complaining of hardships and the danger of starvation in the desert, questioning Moses' competence to lead them to the Promised Land, and doing as they please in a variety of ways — but suffering due and severe punishment for their disobedience and lack of faith. Together with Moses himself they are, as a generation, punished by being denied entry into the land; and many individuals perish in great numbers (e.g., the 14,700 who protested against Moses and Aaron when the earth swallowed up Korah and his 250 associates; Num. 16:35, 49). These incidents and others scattered throughout these books are clearly intended as warnings to a later generation which had already lost the land and suffered great loss of life in consequence of their rebellion against God, but were waiting and hoping for a new dispensation in which God would once again give them unrestricted possession of the land — that is, a second fulfillment of the original promises. That generation undoubtedly believed that God had the power to grant this; but they are warned that obedience to his laws is first required of them. This point is made by implication throughout the narratives of Exodus and Numbers; and in Deuteronomy it dominates the entire book.

In the *patriarchal stories* of Genesis, where it is not a whole people who are portrayed but individuals, the treatment is somewhat different. The patriarchs, even Abraham and Noah, are indeed presented as fallible human beings, and their individual characters, both good and bad, are brought out in some detail. But these are the early days when the promises are newly minted; and the emphasis is not so much on rebellion and punishment as on divine election. One of the leading themes of these accounts is the unexpectedness of the bestowal of God's favor, and in particular of his sovereign choice of improbable individuals to be the heirs of the promises. This is true not only of Abraham, who is chosen out of all mankind to receive the promise, but also of his successors: Isaac, Jacob, and Joseph are all younger brothers whose elders are passed over in their favor. In Gen. 3-11, however, the stories about the sins of Adam and Eve, Cain, the generation of the Flood, and the Tower of Babel emphasize the universal rebelliousness of humanity, although the Flood story itself stresses God's unwillingness to destroy it altogether and offers hope for the future.

God is depicted in the Pentateuch in two ways: as both benevolent and vengeful. These two sides of God's nature are clearly expressed in two passages that stand out from the surrounding text as formal theological statements and so draw attention to themselves as such:

I the Lord your God am a jealous God, punishing children for the iniquity of parents, to the third and the fourth generation of those who reject me, but showing steadfast love to the thousandth generation of those who love me and keep my commandments. (Decalogue: Exod. 20:5-6; Deut. 5:9-10)

The Lord, the Lord, a God merciful and gracious, slow to anger, and abounding in steadfast love and faithfulness, keeping steadfast love for the thousandth generation, forgiving iniquity and transgression and sin, yet by no means clearing the guilty, but visiting the iniquity of the parents upon the children and the children's children, to the third and the fourth generation. (Exod. 34:6-7; cf. Num. 14:18)

These passages are obviously intended to act as both an encouragement and a warning to the readers — and a very severe warning indeed. The readers needed to be reassured that Yahweh's love, so constantly shown in the past in the events recorded in these books, would not now be withdrawn but would continue to be shown in the days to come; and these theological statements offer that reassurance. But the continuance of that love was conditional — it would be given only to those who loved God and kept his commandments.

We cannot know precisely whom the author had in mind as the guilty ones in his own day. However, as some episodes in the narratives show, it must have been difficult to know what was meant by keeping God's commandments. Moreover, although these passages speak of God's forgiving sin and of his being "slow to anger," sinners in the narratives are not always offered the chance to repent and be forgiven. Thus in Exod. 32, as soon as he became aware of the idolatrous making of the Golden Calf and without allowing any possibility of repentance, God immediately determined to destroy the whole people by pestilence, and to start afresh by making Moses, who had taken no part in their sin, into a great nation (v. 10). This is a very strange incident which reveals more than one unexpected side of God's nature. God's threat is averted only by an appeal to him by Moses, who points out the danger to God's reputation if he turns on his own people, and actually has to remind God of his own promises — the oath that he had sworn to Abraham, Isaac, and Jacob (vv. 11-13). There is a similar incident in Num. 14.

Incidents such as these were no doubt intended to send a chill into the hearts of the readers. At the very least they were reminders that the worship of Yahweh was no light matter. Yahweh was a potentially dangerous God whose motives and actions were unpredictable and beyond human comprehension, even inconsistent and changeable. While the people gratefully recognized God's goodwill to those who faithfully served him, it behooved them to be on their guard lest they offend him. Also, not all the punishments inflicted in these stories appear to have been commensurate with the sins committed, as in the case of the "very great plague" causing many deaths inflicted as a punishment for the people's greedy behavior when suddenly provided with quail meat after a long enforced abstinence (Num. 11:31-35).

The Pentateuch and History

In the earlier chapters of this book the question has been raised to what extent, if at all, the events related in the Pentateuch correspond to what actually occurred in sober fact. It is obvious that they cannot entirely correspond. The accounts of the creation of the world in Gen. 1 and 2 belong, if not to the realm of myth, at least to that of cosmological

141

speculation. The creation of the world was observed by no one but God. Again, in Gen. 2 and 3 the term "the man" (Hebrew *ha-adham*), elsewhere denoting the human race, clearly indicates that this story is a symbolic one rather than a factual account of something that actually happened.

So much will be generally agreed by all except for those who hold rigidly to a "literal" interpretation of Scripture — a term that is difficult to define. The matter is different, however, when we come to the other narratives of the Pentateuch, where the individuals mentioned are named. In form, as has been pointed out, many of the patriarchal stories have the characteristics of the folktale. This alone is not sufficient to deny them all historical value. But it has also been pointed out above that it has proved impossible to locate these stories within what is known of the ancient Near East.

The question becomes most acute when we come to the book of Exodus. A later generation of Israelites came to believe that their ancestors underwent a period of slavery and oppression in Egypt and were led out of that land by Moses, were saved from the pursuing Egyptian army by a miracle at the Sea, encountered the god Yahweh at Mount Sinai, where they were given divine laws, and were then guided — more than 600,000 men with their families (Num. 1:46) — through a desert in which they were condemned to travel on foot for forty years, to the border of Palestine in preparation for the occupation of the land.

Granted that this story has been greatly embellished in the telling, is it possible to doubt the historicity of its salient features? Were there no sojourn in Egypt, no Exodus, no miraculous crossing of the Sea, no lawgiving on Sinai, no journey through the desert? It has been suggested that there is some evidence that the historical Israel was mainly indigenous to Palestine and not an immigrant people from outside. However this may be, it is difficult to account for the subsequent development of belief in Yahweh which characterized Israel's subsequent history without allowing for the arrival in Palestine at an early period of a group of people, even if few in number, who came from outside bringing with them the news of a god Yahweh who had miraculously saved them from oppression, which then formed the nucleus of the Pentateuchal story.

To be preoccupied with the question whether the Pentateuch records "history," however, is to miss the point of reading it. In this book I have been — rightly, I believe — concerned not with the Pentateuch's historical accuracy but with its religious lessons; for it was to teach those lessons that the Pentateuch was written. In the Old Testament there are other books which contain profound religious truths expressed in story form. The story of Job is an outstanding example. Like the parables of Jesus, the book of Job does not invite speculation about whether the central figure is a historical person or not. Rather, it is concerned with the nature of God and his world and with the problems of human existence. This is also true in its own way of the Pentateuch, whose teaching I have tried to present in this book.

For Further Reading

Alter, Robert. *The Art of Biblical Narrative.* New York: Basic Books and London: Allen and Unwin, 1981.

Clines, David J. A. *The Theme of the Pentateuch.* JSOT Supplement 10. Sheffield: JSOT Press, 1978.

Douglas, Mary. *In the Wilderness: The Doctrine of Defilement in the Book of Numbers.* JSOT Supplement 158. Sheffield: JSOT Press, 1993.

Driver, Samuel R. *Introduction to the Literature of the Old Testament.* 8th ed. Edinburgh: T. & T. Clark, 1909.

Mayes, A. D. H., *The Story of Israel between Settlement and Exile: A Redactional Study of the Deuteronomistic History.* London: SCM, 1983.

Noth, Martin. *A History of Pentateuchal Traditions.* Englewood Cliffs, N.J.: Prentice-Hall, 1972. Repr. Atlanta: Scholars Press, 1989. (First published in German, 1948.)

Rendtorff, Rolf. *The Problem of the Process of Transmission in the Pentateuch.* JSOT Supplement 89. Sheffield: JSOT Press, 1990. (First published in German, 1977.)

Index

Abraham: history of, 57-58; promises to, 53-57
Alt, Albrecht, 110, 112-13
Alter, Robert, 23
Amphictyony, 19
Apodictic laws, 111, 112-14, 118-19
Archaeology, 134
Astruc, Jean, 13
Atra-ḫasīs, 45-46

Berith. See Covenant
Birth stories, 70-71
Blenkinsopp, Joseph, 42, 71
Blum, Erhard, 22, 51
Book of the Covenant, 118-20

Canaan: commands to kill inhabitants, 92; conquest of, 67-68
Casuistic laws, 111-12, 119
Childs, Brevard, 53
Choice of Israel, God's, 94-95, 96-97
Covenant: second, 7, 97-98; at Sinai, 6, 97, 114; and vassal treaties, 21
Creation stories, 40-42

D source, 23-24

Day, John, 77
Death penalty, 109-10, 112
Decalogue, 6, 113, 115-18
Deuteronomistic History, 2, 85, 91, 96-97, 104, 108-9, 137
Deuteronomy: distinctiveness of, 104; laws of, 120-23; literary style of, 122; monotheism in, 91-92; relationship to other books, 137; speeches in, 6-7; structure of, 86-87; and vassal treaties, 87-88
de Wette, W. M. L., 14-15, 85
Diachronic approach, 135, 136
Dietary laws, 128-29
Documentary Hypothesis, 14-17, 19-20, 23, 134
Dragon and the sea, myth of, 76-77

E source, 23
Eichhorn, Johann Gottfried, 14
Engnell, Ivan, 20
Enuma Elish, 36, 37, 41
Epic of Gilgamesh, 44, 45-46
Etiology, 37-39
Ezra, Ibn, 13

Flood story, 45-47

144